PORTRAIT OF THE TWEED

PORTRAIT
of
THE TWEED

A celebration of the Borders landscape

*

Text and original photography

IAN BAVINGTON JONES

CASSELL

Cassell

Villiers House, 41–47 Strand, London WC2N 5JE

Distributed in the United States
by Sterling Publishing Co., Inc.
387 Park Avenue South, New York, NY 10016–8810

Distributed in Australia
by Capricorn Link (Australia) Pty Ltd
P.O. Box 665, Lane Cove, NSW 2066

British Library Cataloguing-in-Publication data:
A catalogue record for this book is available from the British Library

ISBN 0–304–34220–3

Designed by Ronald Clark

Typeset in Monophoto Palatino by August Filmsetting, St Helens

Printed and bound in Great Britain by
Bath Press, Avon

(*frontispiece*) **Fishing in autumn**

Nigel Limb uses a tethered boat as a casting platform.
Downriver is the famous Upper Floors beat.

To my wife, Jane,
and daughter, Harriet,
and to the memory of my father,
Henry Jones.

ACKNOWLEDGEMENTS

My grateful thanks are due to the many organizations and individuals without whose help this book could not have been published. Firstly, to the various libraries, galleries and collections in England and Scotland that have so efficiently provided of their services. Secondly, to the many people of the Borders who have so generously allowed me access to photograph their houses and land. Special thanks are due, in particular, to Mr Gerald Trotter of Duns, Berwickshire, for his hospitality and for the invaluable local knowledge he was kind enough to share with me. I must also thank Dr Elizabeth McGrath of the Warburg Institute, London, for her time in reading my manuscript and suggesting what were invariably wise changes. Throughout this project I have very much appreciated the enthusiasm and encouragement of my publisher, Cassell. But by far my greatest debt of gratitude is owed to my wife Jane, for the efforts she put into the preparation of the text, and, even more importantly, for always being there with encouragement and faith — *Thank you!*

I.B.J. 1992

CONTENTS

The Tweed Valley and the Borders

1 2 3 4 5 6 7 8 9 10 miles

5 10 15 20 kilometres

EDEN WATER

GLENTRESS FOREST

LEITHEN WATER

GALA WATER

PEEBLES

Neidpath Castle

Mannor Bridge

Kailzie Gardens

STOBO

WALKERBURN

GALASHIELS

Stobo Castle

Dawyck Gardens

INNERLEITHEN

Woollen Mills

Elibank Castle

Ashiestiel
Bridge

CARDRONA
FOREST

Ashiestiel House

ELIBANK AND
TRAQUAIR FOREST YAIR HILL
FOREST

Boleside

Yair House
Yair Bridge

DRUMELZIER PLAIN

Traquair House

MERLINDALE BRIDGE

MANNOR WATER

YARROW WATER

ETTRICK WATER

Newark Castle

STANHOPE

Crook Inn

TWEEDSMUIR KIRK

TALLA RESERVOIR

MEGGET RESERVOIR

ST MARY'S LOCH

ETTRICK WATER

FRUID RESERVOIR

Sheepdog Centre

TWEED'S WELL

Sandy-Knowe, or Smailholm.

View of Smailholm Tower in the Borders, engraved after J.M.W. Turner. From the title page of the 1851 edition of *The Poetical Works of Sir Walter Scott, Bart.*

INTRODUCTION

I T WAS AN ACT OF SERENDIPITY THAT GAVE A FAMILIAR TYPE OF cloth the name of the magnificent River Tweed. A London cloth merchant in the 1830s mistakenly wrote a 'd' for an 'l' when placing an order for Scottish tweel (twill). As the OED definition of the fabric he was ordering — 'of somewhat rough surface and of great variety of texture, originally and still chiefly made in the south of Scotland (usually of two or more colours combined in the same yarn)' — could almost be a description of the river, the name soon became widely used. *Portrait of the Tweed* will look at the country, history, people and fishing that are woven together to produce this most fascinating and beautiful river.

It must be said that Tweed (the definite article should strictly speaking not be used when speaking of the river) is not a wholly Scottish river. Born in Scotland and drawing its life water from a watershed almost entirely Scottish, it runs the first 75 mi (120 km) of its course through Scotland. For the next 19 mi (30 km) from Carham to Paxton, its north bank can still claim to be Scottish but its south bank must admit to being English. And for the last $4\frac{1}{2}$ mi (7 km) from Paxton to Berwick-upon-Tweed, it flows entirely through English soil, as it has done now for over five centuries.

Yet Tweed is not for that reason to be considered a river of uncertain nationality. It is both one of the great Scottish rivers and at the same time the Border river. The Esk and Liddel, on the west coast, are 'border' rivers and as such have their own tales to tell. But the story of the Borders and the history of Scotland belong to Tweed alone.

From the time of the Roman occupation to the Union of the Crowns, when James VI of Scotland (1566–1625) ascended the throne of England in 1603 as James I, Tweed has flowed through the bloody history and destiny of the two countries. The river has been the setting for warring nations, feuding clans and rival families. And this is somehow apt. The word rival, after all, comes from *rivalis* — dweller on a *rivus* (river bank).

Tweed is unique. To follow its course is to journey through history; it is also to admire man's adaptability to circumstance and terrain. From the broad fertile plain inland from Berwick to the rolling country between Kelso and Melrose, through the wooded hills around Peebles to the heather-, bracken- and scree-sided uplands of its birth, Tweed's valley is a potential realized.

A brief history of Tweed and the Borders

I must admit to being uneasy about the relationships of people whose names have a number after them. I am sure I would be able to follow a royal line of straightforward first sons, but half-brothers, intermarriages and bastards render me confused and irritated in about equal measure. I must therefore ask the indulgence of readers who find my précis of Borders history lacking in fine detail and chronological accuracy. What I shall endeavour to do in this brief introductory commentary is to assemble the bare bones of Borders history and to lay flesh upon them in later sections of the book.

It was after the end of the last Ice Age that the Tweed valley was first inhabited by Man. The tribes that moved in from the south and east to colonize were nomadic and territorial. By AD 82 and the arrival of the Romans, the peoples of northern Britain had advanced to being a race with a religion – Druidism. Brass and bronze were replacing stone materials for the production of tools and weapons. There is evidence of the use of horse-drawn chariots in the Borders region. Given the unsuitability of the terrain for such vehicles, it must be assumed that the tribal peoples had yet to acquire the skill of breaking horses. It was these relatively primitive early Britons who faced the might of the advancing Roman armies.

Hadrian's Wall, the best-known bulwark of the Roman Empire in Britain, stretching from the Solway Firth to the mouth of the Tyne, was built around AD 120. It was not, as is so often thought, constructed as the limit of the Empire or to contain those peoples too fierce to quell. It was, in fact, designed to mark the last outposts of civilization. A second wall, running between the Firths of Clyde and Forth 100 mi (160 km) to the north, denoted the effective boundary of the Empire. Although the Romans had ventured as far north as Caledonia, that area did not in their estimation merit the effort involved in holding it.

The land between Hadrian's Wall and its inferior earth and stone counterpart between Clyde and Forth was known to the Romans as the province Valentia. The ferocity and fighting skill of the inhabitants of this province are attested to by the Romans who were stationed there. As with Roman occupations across Europe, much evidence of their presence has remained. Probably the most important archaeological sites are around Newstead, a few miles downriver from Melrose, the true wealth of which was realized only when excavations were made to accommodate the railway in 1843. Finds of Roman remains across the whole area have provided evidence of a purely military occupation with no traces of theatres, baths or temples characteristic of urban settlements. Roman earthworks abound in the area and a particularly striking example of a tumulus or burial mound can be seen on the south bank of Tweed opposite Makerstoun House.

The Dark Ages

With the final abdication of Roman rule and influence, the Borders, like the rest of Britain, sank into the gloom of the Dark Ages. This, more than any other, was a time of mystery and legend. With the exception of the dim candle that illuminated Bede's history, written in Jarrow cAD 730, very little light shines on the truth of those distant centuries. The physical evidence of the Borderers that does remain serves more to confuse than to inform us. The only brough (low, round, dry stone house) to be found outside the northernmost parts of Scotland (where they abound) stands on Torwoodlee Hill on the north bank of Tweed upriver from Galashiels. The proliferation of earthworks in the area is so great as to make it impracticable to map them all, let alone dig and study them. One earthwork dating from the middle centuries of the first millennium that has received much attention is the Catrail. This ditch and ramparted wall of defence, which runs for some 50 mi (80 km) in a north–south direction, appears to have been thrown up to defend mountain-dwellers from the inhabitants of the plains. Not, as one might expect, the other way round.

Arthur, that king of myth and monarch of legend, is said to have dwelt and fought, accompanied by his knightly court, in Tweed Valley. To this day they rest under the Eildon Hills, fully dressed for battle, their horses saddled, awaiting a trumpet call to ride once more to the defence of Scotland. Merlin, too, is associated with the area. Indeed, modern thought, albeit based on dubious evidence, locates his place of burial at Drumelzier on upper Tweed. He was stoned, staked and drowned. It must be assumed, therefore, that he will not be returning.

The most important social change to take place in the Borders was the conversion to Christianity. For a reliable record of this we have the venerated writings of Bede (c672–735). It is possible that towards the end of their occupation, Romans may have introduced the idea of Christianity. But the widespread baptism of the area was performed in the middle of the seventh century by St Cuthbert (d. 687). Originally a shepherd from upper Leader Water, his sanctity was instantly recognized by St Boisil, superior of Mailros (Old Melrose) monastery, who greeted him by proclaiming, 'Behold a servant of the Lord'. Bede's account of the life of St Cuthbert, written in both prose and verse, was drawn from the first-hand accounts of others, Bede himself having been only fourteen or fifteen at the time of Cuthbert's death. The significance for the area of the advent of Christianity was not only spiritual but also artistic and cultural, for it brought with it writing and decoration, as well as building skills and land husbandry.

It was also during the later centuries of the Dark Ages that the separate national identifies of Scotland and England were somehow formed. The kingdom of Northumbria was absorbed into England, and Scotland was soon to be united under one king. The dawning of the second millennium saw the first official designation of Tweed as the border between the two centuries. In the 1018 Malcolm II (c954–1034), known as the Destroyer (a title acquired en route to the Scottish crown), defeated the Northumbrians at the Battle of Carham. From that time until the Union of the Crowns, the line for Anglo-Scottish rivalry was drawn along the course of Tweed.

The bloody road to independence

The wars and battles that were to ravage the area for nearly six centuries soaked the land with the blood of both nations. In the early nineteenth century, the genius of Sir Walter Scott (1771–1832) gave us the Romantic vision of these times in his Border Ballads and Waverley novels. But this portrayal should not mask the cruelty and killing that were to cease only with the unification of the two kindgoms. Of course, there were periods of peace during this time. There were even occasions when the Scots were not fighting among themselves for the right to lead battles against the English, either to regain land lost to them or to extend their southerly border. The great abbeys built in the twelfth century under the pious but far from peaceable King David I (c1082–1153) allowed Saxon architecture a place in the Borders. The thirteenth century, although not without strife, did see growth and prosperity as epitomized by the rise of Berwick under Alexander II (1198–1249) and Alexander III (1241–85). Its success as a port and trading centre led one chronicler, who, it must be said, had probably not seen the original, to describe it as the second Alexandria.

The central issue of the long wars between the kingdoms was Scotland's right to exist as an independent country not subordinate to its English neighbour. The events at the end of the thirteenth century shattered all promise of a civilized and ordered life in the Borders. The accidental death without a male heir of Alexander III in 1285 set the scene for a tragedy that would run with only brief intermissions for more than 300 years. Its leading players formed a *Who's Who* of British history – Edward I, John Balliol, William

Wallace, Robert Bruce, Macbeth, Duncan, Douglas, Edward III, James I, Henry VII, Henry VIII, Mary, Queen of Scots and Elizabeth I.

The absence of a direct heir to the Scottish throne brought forth as many as twenty claimants, the strongest of whom were John Balliol (c1250–1314) and Robert Bruce (1274–1329). After a constitutional crisis which all but broke the Scottish nation, a council of commissioners was convened at Norham in 1296. At this meeting, the commissioners ceded the title of Lord Paramount to Edward I of England (1239–1307) and asked him to adjudicate in the selection of 'their' king, an opportunity for Edward to appoint his

View of Wark Castle, from Scott's *Border Antiquities of England and Scotland* (1815)

puppet. Seventeen months later, in the Great Hall of Berwick Castle, Edward judged in favour of Balliol. Three days after his selection, Balliol paid homage to Edward for the nation of Scotland.

Within four years, however, Balliol attempted to cut the strings that attached him to his master. He allied Scotland to France in her wars against the English. This act, together with an invasion of England, so enraged Edward that he came north to punish Scotland for reneging on her solem oath. His first strike was at Berwick where he killed between 8000 and 15,000 inhabitants, depending on which account is read. For four months he raged through Scotland, asserting his power as Lord Paramount. Although Scotland submitted to Edward, it was to remain a thorn in his side until his death. He had long

View of Melrose Abbey,
from Scott's *Border Antiquities
of England and Scotland* (1815)

View of Kelso Abbey, from
Scott's *Border Antiquities of
England and Scotland* (1815)

stated his desire to make war against no Christian man after beating the Scots. As his death approached, he asked his son to have his heart taken to the Holy Land for burial but his bones kept ready for transportation to all future battles with the Scots. His son failed to comply, and he was buried at Westminster Abbey where his tomb bears the apt inscription 'Malleus Scotorum' (Hammer of the Scots).

Of Edward's three principal Scottish enemies, Balliol is probably the least known, compared with the more renowned Robert Bruce. Within Scotland, however, the honour of national hero is shared between Bruce and Sir William Wallace (c1270–1305).

One small irony associated with this giant among Scottish heroes is his name, which is a corruption of a term for 'Welshman'. Wallace's rise from second son of a relatively low-born family to proclaimed 'Guardian of Scotland' – a title accorded at St Mary's Kirk in 1298 – was short and truly heroic. His place in history was assured by his defeat of the English at Stirling Bridge (1297), when the enemy could not get reinforcements across the bridge because it was jammed with the bodies of their own men. The story of how he made a sword-sling out of a strip of flesh taken from the body of the English treasurer is grotesquely matched by Edward, who, nine months later, having captured and executed Wallace, sent his dismembered limbs for display at Berwick and Roxburgh Castles.

The cudgels to re-establish Scotland were taken up by Robert Bruce. First, he had to establish himself, initially by murdering John, the Red Comyn, in 1306, and then routing the Comyns – a faction loyal to Balliol. Bruce was then free to have himself crowned Robert I at Scone by the Countess of Mar. Of Bruce's many battles that were to lead to a 'free' Scotland, the best remembered is that of Bannockburn in 1314, when Bruce's 5500-strong force defeated the army of Edward II (1284–1327), numbering 20,000 men. Peace was finally confirmed with the marriage of Bruce's son David to Edward III's daughter Joan at Berwick Castle.

Peace was not to be long lived. In 1338, aided and encouraged by Edward III (1312–77), another Balliol seized the Scottish crown and, as a thanks offering to the English king, ceded the Border counties to England. If the previous years had known brief periods of peace, there were to be none in the following 120 years. More destructive for the country than international war, internal power struggles and civil strife further wrecked and retarded the economic growth of the area. The main protagonists were the Crown and the House of Douglas. It was only with the assassination of the eighth Earl of Douglas in 1452 and the exclusion of his family from power that James II (1430–60) could set himself the task of regaining his southern lands. Crucial to his land claim was the retaking of Roxburgh Castle, a task made somewhat the easier for him as the English were otherwise occupied – engaged in their own self-destructive Wars of the Roses. In 1460 James laid siege to Roxburgh. Unfortunately for him, he was keen to see the effect of his new explosive cannon. One of these, having been over-charged, exploded in the barrel, killing him instantly. His wife, Queen Mary, then took command and successfully concluded the siege. While her orders to raze the castle to the ground were being carried out, she had their eight-year-old son crowned James III (1452–88) across the river in Kelso Abbey. James III's reign of twenty-eight years saw little cross-border raiding but was marked by continued inter-Scottish fighting. He was eventually overthrown and murdered, to be replaced by his son James IV (1473–1513). Again, a marriage between two royal families held a promise of peace. Margaret Tudor (1489–1541), daughter of Henry VII and sister of Henry VIII, crossed the border and in 1503 wed James IV.

This marriage could have brought peace to four countries – Scotland, England, France and Spain. But it failed to do so because old enmities and alliances proved stronger than new ones. When Henry VIII (1491–1547) invaded his old enemy, France, in 1513, the French queen called on her old ally, Scotland, for help. In response to the French request, James IV could not resist the chance to tilt once more at his old adversary, England. Such are the circumstances that led, in 1513, to the most pointless and bloody of the defeats of the Scots by the English on Flodden Field beside the River Till, a few miles upstream from its confluence with Tweed. After Flodden, the Scots returned to feuding, largely for the power vested in the guardianship of James V (1512–42), the boy king. James V indeed proved no strong ruler and was by all acounts a weak man, but his reign left three important legacies. The Peel towers that run the whole course of Tweed were already popular with landowners as a first line of defence, but on royal insistence that they be built by all Tweed's landowners, a line of signalling could be set up from Berwick almost to its source. Secondly, for a man who died when only thirty, and who had been a virtual prisoner of his guardians at Stirling Castle for the first fourteen years of his life, James managed to produce a prodigious number of bastards. Many of those from unions with well-born women would later prove a curse on his successors. His final legacy to Scotland, born only a week before his death, was his one legitimate heir, the infant Mary, Queen of Scots (1542–87).

Tudors and Stuarts

It was the sixteenth century and the formidable Henry VIII (1491–1547) sat astride the English throne. Europe was undergoing the trauma of Reformation, as was England, though for different reasons. A female heir to the Scottish throne appeared to afford a

Mary Queen of Scots

For the first, but not the last time, Mary is in mourning. This painting after Clouet shows her in white mourning for the Dauphin of France. *(The Scottish National Portrait Gallery)*

solution to one of Henry's problems. Disregarding historical precedent, he believed that the marriage of the English heir, Edward, to a Scottish queen would give him peace in the north. Not a man of subtlety, he began what was known as the 'Rough Wooing'. His courtship of the Queen's guardians to persuade them of the wisdom of such a union took the form of assaulting Scotland with a ferocity not seen since the black days of Edward I. And, just as with his predecessor, Tweedside was first and hardest hit. The Merse, that area of fertile land surrounding the lower river which had for so long acted as the breadbasket of Scotland, was wrecked. Walter Scott of Branxholm talked of Teviotdale being 'burnt to the bottom of Hell'. A hell with no signs of redemption. The great abbeys of Dryburgh, Kelso, Jedburgh and Melrose were all destroyed by Henry's forces. The young Mary, meanwhile, had been sent to France for her own safety. At the age of fifteen, she married the French Dauphin and was to become Queen of France for seventeen months. In 1561, however, a strong and headstrong young lady of great beauty, she returned to Scotland a widow, not to the Catholic Scotland she had left but to a newly Protestant country, whose church was being led by that misogynistic zealot John Knox. Gifted with charm, beauty and bravery, Mary lacked the cunning and good judgement required to survive in the pit of vipers in which she found herself. Two marriages followed, first to Darnley, Earl of Lennox (1545–67), a Catholic, and, after his murder, to the Earl of Bothwell (c1536–78), her Lieutenant of the Borders, a Protestant. Mary managed to alienate all around her. The Confederate Lords denied her power and held her captive in Lochleven Castle where she was forced to abdicated in favour of her son by Darnley, James.

Following her famous escape in 1568 and her futile attempt to regain the throne with the aid of troops led by Borders lairds, Mary made her last great mistake. She travelled south to England where she threw herself on the mercy of Henry's daughter, the Protestant Elizabeth I (1533–1603). Whether tears were shed or not, Elizabeth signed Mary's death warrant and her eighteen years as a prisoner ended with her execution in 1587.

The final ironic turn of history that was to end the border wars forever came in 1603. On the death of the Virgin Queen, Elizabeth I, Mary's son James VI was, by right of intermarriage between the royal houses, crowned King James I of England. A Scottish king on the English throne. James's move to London deprived Scotland, the oldest kingdom in Europe, of a resident monarch. Scotland was henceforth to be ruled by a Secretary of State. This system of Scottish parliamentary rule from London lasted until the Act of Union was passed in 1707. The Wars of the Covenant which started in 1638 brought Tweed close to being a battle scene again. But for once, the banks of Tweed saw the flow of ink rather than blood. A treaty known as the Pacification of Berwick was drawn up. Although it did not prevent the war, it did allow the forces of King Charles and the Earl of Montrose to go elsewhere to spill each other's blood. For the Borders, generations of warfare and bloodshed were at an end, and even the Jacobite rebellions of the eighteenth century had mercifully little impact on the peace of the region.

View of Traquair House, from Scott's *Border Antiquities of England and Scotland* (1815)

From lawlessness to prosperity

To use a modern expression, the Borders were a 'war zone' for over 150 years. This state of affairs held back the cultural development of its people. It is true that it also bred an individuality and hardiness, but constructive enterprise and artistic endeavour suffered. Moreover, brigandage – on a very widespread scale – was the almost inevitable outcome of centuries of disorder. There can be no other area in Britain that has given the language two words – mosstrooper and reiver – to describe the typical freebooter, robber or villain of those times.

Difficulty in administering law had, as early as 1249, led to the setting up of a code of Borders laws. This statute allowed for the particular Border requirements of a 'hot pursuit' agreement, which also dealt with the thirteenth-century problem of runaway serfs. In the fourteenth century, the whole Borders district was divided into four Marches: East,

Middle and West and the fourth March – the Debatable Land – the area around Liddesdale which was so rife with unsavoury types that it was virtually uncontainable. Justice, or a form of justice, was administered by Wardens. These were very much grace-and-favour appointments, as the Warden of a March was in an enviable position to safeguard his own lands. One imagines, however, that the wardenship of Debatable Land must have been something of a short straw. By the start of the seventeenth century, the Marches had given way to the Middleshires, and the Warden Courts were replaced with the stop-gap of Jethart (Jedburgh) Justice, a judicial system run on the principle of 'Hang first and try later'. Lawlessness in the Borders had always been a problem but now, with the advent of peace, its suppression assumed a new sense of urgency.

Attempts were made to reform the ways of the Borders as early at 1605. A commission consisting of five Englishmen and five Scotsmen was charged with the unenviable task of taming the Borderers. One of their directives – almost biblically – instructed the owners of houses protected by large iron gates to turn those gates into ploughs.

The perennial Borders crime of smuggling could be dealt with easily by introducing a common duty between Scotland and England. Meanwhile, the reivers and mosstroopers, much romanticized in later times, were in fact dreaded and dreadful masters of unorganized crime throughout the region. They were eventually to be eradicated by being subjected to the same methods of violence and intimidation that they had employed in their nefarious work.

One immediate problem posed by the ending of hostilities between England and Scotland and the gradual establishment of law was widespread unemployment. Soldiering and stealing had always provided work for the men of the Borders, but these occupations had now gone. So began a tradition of emigration and, on occasion, deportation. For the next 300 years, people would leave their Borders homes to build new lives across the globe. Canada, the USA, South Africa and New Zealand all have their Berwicks, Coldstreams, Kelsos, Melroses and Peebles – reminders of the people who left the banks of Tweed to start again in the frontierlands of new worlds beyond the sea.

The Agricultural Revolution in the Borders

During the centuries of war, wealth had been vested in land and in men: the men to fight and the land to feed them. With slowly growing trust came the realization that money was the new currency and agriculture the means of generating it. Sheep had first been introduced by the Cistercian monks at Melrose in the twelfth century and crops of grain had been grown on the rich soil of the Merse for almost as long as man had occupied it.

New systematic farming methods had to be adopted if profits and employment were to be increased. In 1723 a Society for Improving in the Knowledge of Agriculture was set up. This acted as a forum for the exchange of ideas, both those of local farmers and published works from other areas. New crops were introduced – potatoes from the Americas and the swede from Scandinavia which, to the constant confusion of the English, is known as the 'neep'. A Mr Jackson of Kelso took advantage of the American War of Independence and grew a very profitable crop of tobacco on his farm. Others followed suit and the following year many thousands of acres of Borders land were planted likewise. Late spring and summer storms did not help this tender crop, which in any case was finally bought and destroyed by the Crown which, on the advice of its lawyers, withdrew Scotland's colonial trading rights.

Different breeds of livestock were introduced: Blackface sheep and Cheviot sheep for their quality fleeces and lamb production, and Short Horn cattle that were found to be most productive and sufficiently hardy. Many of the fine Georgian houses in Edinburgh's New Town were built with the profits from Borders farming.

In his survey of Roxburghshire in 1798, Douglas notes that there is 'very inconsiderable' manufacture of cloth, but observes the large numbers of sheep and excellent supply of water for powering machines. Small-scale cloth production had for a long time taken place throughout the Borders, but was mainly for local consumption. Most of the wool produced had been baled and exported. It was probably the sudden need for uniforms to clothe the British Army in the Napoleonic Wars that gave the necessary impetus to start large-scale cloth production on Tweedside. The locally produced wool was augmented with fleeces brought down from the Highlands, which at this time were undergoing mass clearances. Flemish craftsmen were encouraged to settle in the area to bring their skills to the new industry. The great latent power of Tweed and its tributaries was harnessed to work the looms that would rattle and clatter along its length. The nineteenth and early part of the twentieth centuries saw Tweed at the high point of its cloth production. Cheap imports and man-made fabrics have reduced the woollen industry to a shadow of its former self, although quality rather than quantity keeps the world-renowned names of Pringle, Lyle & Scott, Braemar and Ballantyne employed. Thus, a long period of warfare, pacification, agricultural prosperity, manufacturing evolution (and manufacturing decline) has produced the Borders we know today – a landscape which, for innumerable visitors each year, represents the enduring traditions of rural life.

The sporting scene

Whether they are pronounced 'Hunting, Shooting and Fishing' or 'Huntin-Shootin-an-Fishin', for these activities Tweed and its valley are without peer. The provision of woods and coverts among the rolling hills of middle Tweed allow for some of the finest pheasant shoots in the country. The heather-covered grouse moors of the upper river are a match for any of their Highland or Yorkshire counterparts. Surtees's great huntsman Jorrocks could have found no better hunting country than that beside the lower river. But it is the fishing above all else that sets Tweed apart.

Tweed For Ever

Let ither angler choose their ain,
An' either waters tak' the lead
O'Wielan streams we covet nane
But gi'e to us the bonnie Tweed
An' gi'e to us the cheerfu burn
That steals into its valley fair —
The streamlets that at ilka turn
Sae softly meet an' mingle there.

THOMAS TOD STODDART 1866

The world over, fishermen talk of Tweed. It is well known that Tweed's fishing accounts for a large percentage of the tourist trade in the area. Quite how large is very difficult to say. For every visitor intent on fishing Tweed, I suspect there are many more travellers to Scotland who simply choose to break their journey 'oh, somewhere around Kelso, by the way'.

At this point I should explain that the term 'fisherman' is not used with the intention of excluding women. It simply implies one who fishes, regardless of gender. I will however in this and later fishing sections refer to a person who fishes as a Rod. Non-fishing readers may find it hard to understand quite why people choose to spend large sums of money for the privilege of standing waist-deep in cold running water. Yet no portrait of Tweed could exist without an account of the life-cycle of the salmon which is so closely interlinked with it — and the thrall it holds over the thousands of visitors who come to fish its waters.

Fox hunting

Towards the end of the spring season hunts work the upper, more wooded areas of the Tweed valley, leaving the sheep and lambs on the lower ground undisturbed. These hounds belong to the Duke of Buccleuch's Hunt.

It is a long tradition on Scottish rivers that 'a fish' is a salmon unless otherwise stated. To paraphrase an old saying, 'which came first, the salmon or the egg?' In this instance the answer is the egg. The female salmon – the *hen* – settles on a suitable spawning ground or *redd*. These redds are areas of clean, silt-free gravel, in which Tweed abounds from the uppermost reaches of its watershed down to the upper tidal level. Having created a trough in the gravel with her tail, she pairs up with a male fish, the *cock*. Lying just above the trough, she carefully extrudes her eggs which the cock fertilizes by engulfing them in a cloud of melt. Once this is complete, she covers the eggs with gravel for their protection. Thin and weak after breeding, both cock and hen, now know as *kelts*, attempt to make their way back downriver. Most will be unsuccessful and die before reaching the sea.

Spawning takes place from November to January. A few months after fertilization, tiny *alevins* emerge from amongst the gravel. They quickly develop into *fly*, then a year later into *parr*. For the next two to four years they will live in the river, feeding on aquatic flies and larvae. In the late spring and early summer of their third or fourth year, depending on how successful their feeding has been, the parr lose their distinctive 'finger' markings and drop downriver to enter the salt waters of the sea as *smolts*. At sea they become voracious feeders, eating shrimps, prawns, sand eels, herring and plankton, and travel prodigious distances to feeding grounds off Greenland and Newfoundland. The time spent at sea varies between one and four years. A fish that returns after one winter is known as a *grilse*, any longer than this and it is known as a *salmon*.

It is one of life's wonderful mysteries that, having travelled many thousands of miles across the Atlantic Ocean, a mature salmon can find its way back to the river of its birth – or, to be more accurate, the river it left as a smolt. Parr born in one river and released into another will invariably return to the river from which they entered the sea. But although their metabolism is able to make the initial change from fresh to saltwater feeding, the reverse process does not occur. So their journey upriver is made with an empty belly and they must live on their reserves of fat. Depending on when they re-enter the river, fishermen known them as *spring*, *summer* or *autumn fish*. Yet, regardless of when they return to the river, they will wait until November, December or January to make their redds and start the cycle over again.

The hen lays between 2000 and 15,000 eggs, but what percentage of these survive to come back as salmon is not known. Nature, of course, allows for a high mortality rate, and survival is threatened by two groups – natural predators and man. The former comprises birds (cormorants, gulls, goosanders, herons, shags and osprey), fish (eels, chub, perch, pike and trout) and mammals, (mink and otter), all of which prey on salmon in their various stages while in freshwater. At sea the greatest natural predator of salmon is the grey seal, which kills many thousands of fish and injures many more each year. In freshwater, too, disease may be responsible for very high death rates among mature fish. Ulcerative dermal necrosis (UDN) can reach epidemic proportions. It leaves its wretched victims covered with fungus to die in the river's backwaters, often within sight of spawning grounds they lack the strength to reach.

Man's predatory activities are more sinister and far-reaching. Industrial pollution can ruin a river and destroy its animal inhabitants. Fortunately, Tweed can boast the cleanest river system in Britain. With the decline of cloth mills and the environmentally responsible approach of those that remain, industrial effluent is no longer the problem it was once, although there is no room for complacency. A new threat, however, is land usage in the river's catchment area. Afforestation and water abstraction, combined with heavy rain, can flood the system with silt, thus disturbing and smothering the redds. Damming the upper tributaries to form reservoirs for water-supply schemes may reduce the main river's flow and exclude salmon from some of their spawning grounds.

Commercial fishing, both legal and illegal, takes a heavy toll on salmon stocks. The number of river nets which at one time stretched as far upriver as Norham has been greatly reduced in recent years, as has their season. Sadly, deep-sea fishing over the feeding grounds, which is controlled by a quota, and the cruel and illegal drift or gill nets still account for a huge number of Tweed-bound fish. On the other hand, since the number of rod-caught salmon represents only a single-figure percentage of fish taken from the river, rod fishing cannot be considered as a threat to fish stocks.

There are several requirements to sustain a healthy salmon stock, as dictated by the life-cycle of the fish. Fresh, clean, well-oxygenated water – Tweed has 97 mi (155 km) of it, plus many hundreds of miles of feeder streams; good breeding grounds – virtually the whole river system; food supply for the immature fish – because of Tweed's lowland position and relatively short winter, this is plentiful; and fish runs – salmon enter Tweed throughout the whole year. Other rivers share these features, but Tweed has them in abundance. There is rich variety in its *pools* – from the long deep runs and *dubs* of the broad lower river flowing across the vibrantly rich Merse, through to the faster middle river, first gliding, then turning and tumbling as it makes its way through the Arcadian beauty of its valley; and on to the tighter, rockier upper river, twisting down through the heather and bracken-sided hills. All rivers can be found in Tweed.

The noble salmon

Salmon have been fished for sport since the middle of the seventeenth century. It was the advent of rod rings and reels that allowed the pursuit of the salmon, for a simple line affixed to the end of a pole was never a match for such a powerful fish. Tackle and techniques were refined to a high degree of perfection in the nineteenth century, so that today's fly fisherman uses much the same principles and equipment as his Victorian predecessor — although tackle now makes use of the most modern materials. Fishing rods of 15–20 ft (5–6 m) are now made of lightweight carbon fibre and are considerably less cumbersome than their old greenheart and hickory predecessors. Modern reels machined from aluminium carry scientifically designed plastic-coated lines and have replaced heavy brass reels and dressed silk lines.

In fly fishing, the fly itself, which has relatively little weight, is projected by the heavier, tapered line to the point where the fisherman wants it placed. Silkworm gut was formerly employed to attach the fly to the flyline. This has now been replaced by stout nylon. The flies used today tend to be a combination of fur and feather tied either directly on to a hook or on to a shank or tube which then has a hook attached. The gloriously elaborate flies so prized by Victorian and Edwardian fishermen are seldom used these days. Although works of art, their complicated designs often called for the use of feathers from birds which are now either extinct or endangered. (It must be stressed that this sad state of affairs was not brought about by wild-eyed fly dressers — the feathers were merely a by-product of the then-thriving millinery trade.) Modern tackle has not made it easier to catch fish but has made it possible to walk unaided back to the hotel at the end of a day's fishing.

One of Tweed's many idiosyncrasies is that it does not have any gillies — it has boatmen, whose job it is to assist the fishermen. As their title implies, they often take their Rods in a boat on to the wider sections of the river to try for fish that could not be covered with a fly or bait by the wading angler. For some years I have had the pleasure of fishing with Mr Eain Fairgreave on Makerstoun Water. He epitomizes a good Tweed boatman: mastery of the oars, an encyclopedic knowledge of his water, boundless enthusiasm and, above all, first-rate company.

Special legislation to deal with salmon fishing on the Border river dates back to 1771. In 1857 the Tweed Fisheries Act called for the setting up of the River Tweed Commissioners. This commission, comprising representatives of the Crown, commercial fisheries companies, estate owners and syndicates, still controls and regulates salmon fishing on

Tweed. The commissioners set the season, regulate the fishing methods and supervise the maintenance and welfare of the river.

Since man first occupied the river valley until the present day, and, one hopes, long into the future, Tweed's one constant resource has been that most noble of fish — the salmon. It has been taken to feed itinerant farmers and to sustain troops. It has been netted in vast numbers to be boiled, barrelled and shipped from Berwick. And today it is pursued and prized as the most worthy of sporting fish. For countless generations the salmon have returned to the river of their birth to breed. They, in truth, constitute Tweed's oldest family. So, with due reference to their seniority, we shall emulate their behaviour and follow the river upstream.

Boat fishing

Holding a boat in position is made to look easy by skilled Tweed Boatmen. However, river flow is surprisingly strong and the "right" position is only known with intimate knowledge of the water.

EARLY SPRING

Tweedmouth to Carham Hall

Berwick Lighthouse (1) • Berwick Viaduct (2) • Paxton House (3)
Norham Castle (4) • Ladykirk Kirk (5) • Norham and Ladykirk Bridge (6)
Twizel Castle and Bridge (7) • Flodden Field (8)
Coldstream Bridge (9) • The Hirsel (10) • Wark Castle (11)
Birgham (12) • Carham Church (13)

Berwick Lighthouse

Berwick harbour is never easy to enter. The lighthouse aids sailors to chart a course through treacherous sandbanks.

THIS, THE FIRST STRETCH OF RIVER, TO BE VIEWED IN EARLY spring, runs from the salty water of Tweed's mouth at Berwick to an almost anonymous point about $\frac{3}{4}$ mi (1 km) downstream from Eden Hall. Anonymous but highly significant, for it is there that Tweed becomes a wholly Scottish river. The cartographer's line is, no doubt, accurately drawn; but as all the people who live along the valleys of Tweed are Borderers, I shall not be bound by the Ordnance Survey's demarcations. All of Tweed is the Border river.

The low hills and wide fields that slope down to the river, together with the couple of towns and few small villages that stand beside it, are deceptive. Although they appear gentle and comfortable, their past is betrayed by their names – Berwick, Coldstream, Carham, Birgham, Norham, Wark, Twizel and Flodden. No other section of the river can claim such a bloodstained history. The apparent calm of the area confounds its past. Of course, Berwick's fortifications are there for all to see, and there are castle ruins liberally dotted along the river. Picturesque as they are, however, they are false persuaders. They would have us believe that their tales are solely of romance and valour, belying the acts of barbarism and treachery that brought them into existence and finally laid them waste. This is a most charming and fertile land but its stories are not for the squeamish.

These are the last $23\frac{1}{2}$ mi (37 km) of Tweed's long journey. The river's course finishes in long, lazy meanders – a mellow contrast to the strength and impatience of the middle and upper reaches. Islands now form where all debris would once have been pushed aside to the banks. Vast as the river is, carrying water from some 1500 sq mi (4000 sq km) of catchment area, it is no match for the tide, the effect of which is felt over 4 mi (6.5 km) upstream from the river's mouth. The lower Tweed's stately course proceeds through the soft, rolling countryside of Berwickshire and Northumberland. This is excellent farming land, its large, regular fields marked out with neat hedges or fences. Land of this quality is too valuable to allow for much woodland; still, in the interests of shooting and hunting, some coverts and small woods are preserved.

Even with our backs firmly to the North Sea, February on the 'early spring' section of the river can be inhospitable. The raw wind that seems to blow constantly has none of its edge removed by the leafless trees. The rain, sleet and snow can swell the already broad river to frightening proportions. Even the rich dark soil of the Merse takes on an almost demonic blackness. Yet, despite what our senses tell us, this is indeed spring. Tiny buds are forming on bare branches, land is being prepared for planting and salmon are coming in from the sea to start their homeward journey. The new year has begun.

Just where Tweed ends and sea begins depends on the state of the tide. At low tide the river maintains its identify beyond Berwick Lighthouse, while at high tide, particularly spring high tides, the sea appears to bully itself well above Berwick Bridge.

'The frontier regions of most great kingdoms, while they retain that character, are unavoidably deficient in objects of antiquary.' So wrote Walter Scott in the introduction to his *Border Antiquities* (1815). Broadly speaking, he is right. Nevertheless, Berkwick-upon-Tweed is itself of great antiquity. It is no longer as great as it once was – the castle has all but gone and the harbour that formerly serviced a royal fleet is now used to house a small fishing fleet and a lifeboat station – but it is still a fine old fortified town, and, indeed, the only one on Tweed to have survived relatively intact.

The royal city of Berwick

The first certain mention of Berwick dates from as early as 872, when the Pictish King Gregory, or Grig, made the small fishing village his quarters before travelling south to sack Lindisfarne. Although little is known of the growth from village to town, Berwick was well established by 1018 and the Battle of Carham. Malcolm II (*c*954–1034), the Scottish victor, was keen to see Berwick strengthened and developed, realizing its significance as the key point of entry to Scotland. By 1040, Duncan, best known for his subsequent assassination that same year by Macbeth (d. 1057), had been able to use Berwick to fit out eleven battleships.

The next two and a half centuries saw continued growth and expansion, as well as changing ownership. At the start of the thirteenth century, King John of England (1167–1216) burned and sacked the town twice, but it recovered its prominence under Alexander II (1198–1249) and Alexander III (1241–85). The export trade in hides, wool and salmon must have been very profitable. In 1286 the town paid £2190 in customs dues to the Scottish Exchequer. This figure may seem modest today but then it represented one-quarter of the total customs of England. In addition to what it sent abroad, the port also landed cargoes from Europe. Alexander III's supply of wine certainly entered through Berwick, and records show him owing a Gascon merchant £2000. Comparing the wine bill with the duty bill, it must be assumed either that the king had vast cellars or that the wine was exceedingly expensive or that the customs duty was very low.

The trade in wool and hides was largely generated by the abbeys, not just in the Borders but throughout Scotland. Tithes were paid both in money and produce. Fresh salmon, obviously, could not be exported. They were boiled in a special solution of brine, the composition of which was a closely guarded secret, known only to the coopers who did the boiling and barrelling. Some live fish could be sent to other markets, and indeed boats with wells were built for the purpose. The fish had to be transferred from the nets quickly and voyage times kept as short as possible to avoid a spoilt cargo. The 'modern' practice of packing salmon in ice for shipment began in 1788. This brought to an end the large cooperage trade in the town.

Devastation and decline

The death of Alexander III and that of his only possible heir, Margaret, Maid of Norway (c1282–90), saw the beginning of Berwick's violent decline. Edward I (1239–1307) of England chose John Balliol (c1250–1314) to be king of Scotland in the Great Hall of Berwick Castle on 17 November 1297. Four years later, Edward returned to Berwick, furious at Balliol's refusal to act as his puppet. Although Edward was to ravage Scotland in his pursuit and humiliation of Balliol, it was the town of Berwick-upon-Tweed that suffered the greatest outrage. The English king personally supervised the slaughter of the inhabitants, calling a halt, it is said, only after witnessing a woman in the act of childbirth being put to the sword. The corpses were left to rot. After four months, with Balliol banished to France, Edward brought the landowners, lairds and bishops down to 'Stinking Berwick' to sign the Ragman Roll. In later years this name was to be corrupted to 'rigmarole', but it was no long-winded, meaningless threat that persuaded the Scots to sign supremacy over to the English king. It was only after the victory of Robert Bruce (1274–1329) at Bannockburn in 1314 that Berwick again came under Scottish control.

On 25 August 1482, the town changed hands for the thirteenth and last time. With the Union of the Crowns in 1603, Berwick Castle lost its status as a garrison. Less than forty years later, the Earl of Suffolk sold the structure to the corporation, which used it as a quarry for church building. In 1843 the North British Railway Company bought the site and blew up what remained of the castle to make way for the Royal Border Bridge and Station. Passengers buying their tickets at Berwick are standing on the spot where King Edward I decided in favour of Balliol many centuries earlier.

The ecclesiastical history of Berwick is as nothing compared with that of Melrose or Kelso. It has never boasted an abbey or monastery. The great Border abbeys did at one time own property in the town, but that was to serve their secular interests of trade and commerce. It is apt that the spire jutting out over the roofline should belong not to the parish church but to the Town Hall.

The living past

The narrow streets and stone buildings of Berwick heighten the sense of being in a small medieval town. Of course, the street plan and appearance have altered over the seven centuries since Berwick was one of the most important trading centres in northern Europe. But only a little imagination is needed to see how it must once have been, either as a flourishing port and market or a strongly defended garrison town at the very heart of the Border Wars.

Berwick is still a town of bridges, walls and roofs. Tweed's first bridge stands barely above the shoreline: a low, narrow construction with buttresses that also serve as refuges for foot passengers. First opened to traffic in 1624, it has over the years afforded equally safe passage across the river to horses, carts and motor cars. The need for a wider, more efficient crossing was met in the early twentieth century with the building of a new triple-span road bridge, a few hundred yards up from its older counterpart. But by far the most spectacular of Berwick's bridges is the rail viaduct that conveys the main East Coast Line. It was built at the prodigious cost of more than a quarter of a million pounds. Aptly described as standing 'between the Tweed and the clouds', it dwarfs all around it, a total of twenty-eight arches spanning the 2152 feet (700 metres) from the firm ground on the south bank to the railway station just above the town.

The walls that now encase Berwick date from the reign of Elizabeth I (1533–1603). Their design and construction were supervised by Italian engineers who used as their models the ramparted walls of Verona and Antwerp. Whether more solidly built or less in demand for defence, Berwick's walls remain while those upon which they were drawn have long since been destroyed.

In contrast to the darkened stone walls are the red pantiled roofs of the town. Pantiles or Flemish tiles were widely imported from the Low Countries in the eighteenth century. It was from the trade in pantiles that the great Adam family of architects amassed its fortune, affording young Robert Adam (1728–92) the leisure to travel around Europe studying classical architecture. For Berwick, it re-established a link that went back to the thirteenth century when Flemish traders and merchants were encouraged to settle in the town to stimulate commerce with the Continent.

The next crossing point of Tweed above Berwick is the recent road bridge that carries the speeding traffic of the Great North Road (A1). Just above the bridge, Tweed is joined by its last main tributary, the Whiteadder. An attractive little river, it flows through a pretty valley from its source in the Lammermuir Hills. At one time many castles stood along Whiteadder's banks. Of these, only Cranshaws remains. A mile or so above Whiteadder Point, the river is beyond the mean high-water mark. Although some small tidal effect can be felt, the river no longer reveals ugly mud flats at low tide. Shortly after the high-water mark, Tweed becomes the national boundary. For the next 19 mi (30 km) the banks are referred to as English (south) or Scottish (north). The first significant feature is on the Scottish bank. On the outside of a great slow bend of the river, amongst the first woodland of any size, stands Paxton House. This most dignified Robert Adam house is set high above the river, its pale stone contrasting with the surrounding trees. The interiors include the dramatically proportioned Picture Gallery.

A fine view of Paxton House downriver and Horncliffe House upriver on the English bank can be had from the Union Suspension Bridge – the first suspension bridge to be built in Britain. It was designed by Captain Samuel Brown RN and built in 1820. Its narrow track, tall towers and fine black chains gainsay its undoubted strength. When it was built it was the only safe crossing between Berwick and Coldstream. Horncliffe is the first village of any size after Berwick and stands a little above and back from the river on the English side. It seems to have been relatively untouched by the fighting that has scarred so much of the rest of the lower river. Close by, in the middle of the river, St Thomas's Island is Scottish. The national boundary runs through the stream on its English side. The Island stands up to 20 ft (6 m) above the river and so is protected from even the strongest spring tide which can just about be detected this far upstream.

Berwick Viaduct

The substantial pillars of the great rail viaduct whose construction required the further destruction of the remains of Berwick Castle.

Norham: a dangerous place

Norham is a very tranquil little village halfway between Berwick and Coldstream. It has a few shops, a post office, a public house at each end of the main street, a police station and an old church, much rebuilt in the nineteenth century. In the middle of the wide village green stands a cross which dates from the last century, although its base is said to be very much older. Nestled snugly into the inside of a bend on the English side of the river, it appears quite a rural village in the heart of some particularly fine, gentle farming land. Yet Sir Walter Scott (1771–1832) described it as the most dangerous place in Britain.

On any river, an easy crossing will attract settlement. Tweed being a Border river, fordable places also assumed a strategic importance and became points of defence. The old name for Norham was Ubbanford and it was a ford well worth defending. At high

Eyemouth (*right*)

Standing on the Berwickshire coast, the salt harbour of Eyemouth has developed into a busy fishing port and holiday resort. In contrast the difficult tidal currents and shifting sandbanks of Berwick have helped to reduce the ancient town's economic importance.

Berwick (*left*)

The pantiled roofs, town walls and bridges of the ancient town contrast with the mixture of salt and freshwater of Tweed as it enters the sea.

water, especially when swollen with February rain, the wide, slow, coloured water of Tweed around Norham would have been impassable to foot traffic. But at low water, as attackers soon realized, it was possible for anyone with local knowledge to wade or ride across with more safety than at any previous point. As a regular crossing point it was unreliable, but not until 1839, two centuries after Norham's importance began to wane as a result of the Union, was it replaced by the robust stone Ladykirk and Norham Bridge.

Norham Castle stands just outside the village, perched, almost overhanging the river, on top of a 100-ft (33-m) steep bank. Although in a state of considerable ruin, it is by far the most intimidating and forbidding castle on Tweed. It is enclosed on its river side by trees, and at dawn colonies of crows leave the bare black branches to circle the ruins, as if still hoping to find the rich pickings of carrion that for so long accompanied the castle's occupation.

Norham played a crucial part in almost all the important episodes of Border history. In 1121 Bishop Flambard (d. 1128) replaced the old fortifications with what was to be the nucleus of the present ruins. It was built to be impregnable, yet David I (c1082–1153) took and destroyed it only seventeen years after its completion. Bishop Pudsey, also of Durham, rebuilt the castle on the same site, strengthening the walls and erecting the great tower, some of which still remains. In 1215, the same year as he signed Magna Carta, King John I laid siege to Norham in one of his many battles with his own barons. After forty days, with no hope of success, he withdrew. Edward I used the castle as his royal residence when acting as arbitrator in the disputed accession to the Scottish throne. It was to Norham that his choice, John Balliol, came to pay the homage of Scotland to Edward. In the years from its first building in 1121 until the Union of the Crowns, the castle fell to the Scots only four times and they never occupied it for more than a few weeks. The perimeter wall was always large enough to house many of the villagers of Norham at times of siege. But by leaving the village undefended it was invariably sacked and burned. The last Scot to hold Norham was King James IV (1473–1513), who took the castle in his victorious run-up to Scotland's spectacular defeat at Flodden.

Although Scott gave such a dire warning of the danger of Norham, he also gives a wonderfully romantic impression of it. The first stanza of his epic poem *Marmion* (1808) describes the castle at the height of its defensive power.

Day set on Norham's castled steep,
And Tweed's fair river, broad and deep,
And Cheviot's mountains lone:
The battle towers the donjon keep,
The loophole gates, where captives weep,
The flanking walls that round it sweep,
In yellow luster shone.
The warriors on the turrets high,
Moving athwart the evening sky,
Seem's forms of giant hight.
Their armour, as it caught the rays,
Flash'd back again the western blaze,
In lines of dazzling light.

Almost directly across the river from Norham village lies the hamlet of Ladykirk. Prior to 1500 it was called Upsettlington. Edward I met eight of the claimants to the Scottish throne there; he also, in negotiation with the Scottish nobility, tried to settle the Balliol-Bruce feud. As its name implies, Ladykirk has a church dedicated to the Virgin Mary but little else. But it is a lovely church, built on the direct instructions of James IV to give thanks to the Virgin on his being saved from drowning in Tweed. It is built on a cruciform plan with a nave nearly 95 ft (29 m) long. Constructed of local red sandstone, it seems almost to glow when viewed in a low morning or evening light. It is remarkable that a church built right on the Border and dedicated to the Virgin Mary less than half a century before the Reformation has remained completely intact.

Midway between Norham and Coldstream, Tweed is joined by the River Till. The Till is entirely English. Born in the Cheviot Hills, it picks an eccentric course through Northumberland before entering Tweed besides the ruins of St Cuthbert's Chapel. The lower reaches of Till are almost canal-like. There appears to be very little current and the stream is not particularly wide. But like so much in the area, this is deceptive. The current has strength, the edges of the steam are deeper than the middle and the river bed, which contains very few rocks, is apt to give way underfoot. An age-old rhyme gives due warning of Till's menace.

Says Tweed to Till
'What gars ye rin sae still?'

Says Till to Tweed
'Although ye run wi' speed
And I rin slow,
For ae man that ye droon
I droon twa!'

It was the Till, or rather the bridge over the Till at Twizel, that played a crucial part in the defeat of the Scots by the English at the Battle of Flodden in 1513. By crossing the larger body of his troops over Twizel Bridge, the Earl of Surrey was able to place his men at the foot of Branxton Hill. James IV had seen a smaller section of English moving to his north and had dispatched Lord Home to deal with them. Home duly overran the enemy force with his cavalry. But Surrey had placed the main body of his troops in Flodden Field on the steep Tweed side of Branxton Hill not – as James had expected – on the gentler Till side slopes. By forcing James to charge down into Flodden Field, Surrey effectively denied the Scots both their cavalry and cannon. The outcome was a crushing defeat for the Scots and the death of James and his seventeen-year-old-son Alexander, Archbishop of St Andrew's.

Coldstream: site of war and peace

Coldstream is on the Scottish bank, but only just. The high retaining wall that runs straight up from the water's edge barely manages to keep the town on Scottish soil. Like Norham, Coldstream developed because of its ford. Although it was a much safer option than its downstream counterpart, it was still subject to the vagaries of the river's flow. One rather humble old inn in the town was a temporary abode of many royal visitors waiting for the river to subside. The noble and beautiful bridge, designed by John Smeaton (1724–92) and opened in 1766, did away with the ford. Today the bridge is as well used as it ever was, carrying cars and lorries that thunder across from Cornhill-on-Tweed up and through the town. Just below the bridge, Tweed gently rolls over Coldstream Cauld and only through the fish pass, on the English side, does the water show any sign of the strength of the current. Until an Act of Parliament put a stop to such things, the toll house on the Scottish side of the bridge was as well known for its irregular marriages as the blacksmith's shop in Gretna Green – 'many cursed the day they crossed the Tweed for such a purpose'. The fact that Gretna Green, rather than Coldstream, is renowned for its runaway marriages is simply because Coldstream has more significant claims to fame.

Despite the busy A697 that runs straight through its centre, Coldstream is a neat and well-kept little town. Its public gardens have a fine show of colour throughout the year. The immediately surrounding countryside still has the characteristic gentle roll of the lower river, but more trees and woods are now in evidence.

Being as 'on the Border' as it is possible to be, Coldstream had a continual involvement in the Border Wars. At a time when a place was defined by its parish, Coldstream was a part of Lennel, and it was with the near-total destruction of Lennel in the Border Wars that Coldstream itself became a parish. Edward I used the ford to enter Scotland in order to continue the destruction of the nation that had begun in Berwick. From that time onward, Coldstream witnessed the repeated cross-Border advances and retreats of the rival armies — and often received equally harsh treatment from both.

For a place that experienced so much warfare, it seems fitting that it was also the site of the last truce signed between England and Scotland. In 1489, a five-year truce was made in the names of James IV and Henry VII (1457–1509). This did not reflect a common hope of Anglo-Scottish peace between the monarchs; it was simply to allow a mutually advantageous break from Border fighting. James of Scotland had internal problems, mainly from his Highland chiefs, while Henry was engaged in England's age-old battle with the French. The Union of the Crowns saw an end to the Border Wars, but it did not result in the long-term withdrawal of a military presence from Coldstream. In 1659, General Monk raised a regiment of foot guards at Coldstream – the Coldstream Guards – which he marched south to help restore Scottish Stuart monarchy to the British throne.

The ecclesiastical history of Coldstream dates back to 1165 when Cospatric of Dunbar founded a Cistercian priory, which endured until it was completely destroyed by the first Earl of Hertford in 1545. During the reign of Henry VIII (1491–1547) a papal legate published a bull in Coldstream against the printing of the Scriptures. Yet, in defiance of the bull, albeit 300 years later, Dr Adam Thomson set up a printing house, on the site of the old priory, for the production of cheap Bibles.

Coldstream's counterpart on the English side is Cornhill-on-Tweed. The castle at Cornhill was long a target of Scottish raids. It was demolished in 1385, then rebuilt, only to be demolished and looted again in 1549. There is a most attractive church at Cornhill, constructed, almost defiantly, in the English style. Post-Union cooperation prevailed in the nineteenth and twentieth centuries when Coldstream was served by Cornhill's railway station.

A little way above Coldstream, beside the River Leet, stands the Hirsel – residence of the Homes of the Hirsel. The attractive flat-fronted house is built of almost white stone from local quarries. Its extensive grounds are planted with a variety of specimen trees which are complemented by the vast array of rhododendrons and azaleas, seen at their splendid best in May and June. The man-made Hirsel Lake is the only lake of any size along the length of the lower river: the good natural drainage of the area usually feeds all excess water directly into Tweed. The Homes (Hume being the old spelling and present pronunciation) have been an influential family in the Borders as long as there has been a border. That the line has survived testifies not only to the military acumen of earlier members, but also to the ability of more recent Homes to adapt to changing circumstances. The name of the present family seat, the Hirsel, means 'sheepfold': and it was through farming that the Homes prospered after the Union with England. An elegant country estate would have been of little use before peace was firmly established in the area. In those days Home Castle was a more suitable abode. Despite many raids and sieges, the castle only once fell to the English, in 1547, but was retaken by the Homes in 1549. It was battered into surrender by the Earl of Sussex in 1569 and finally demolished by Colonel Fenwick, acting for Cromwell, in 1650.

Tiny villages: momentous events

The last three places worthy of mention in this lower section of the river are Wark, Carham and Birgham. Together they never mustered more than a few hundred souls, but each in its time was of pivotal importance to the history of a nation.

The diminutive village of Wark stands hard by Tweed on the English side. Its few houses line the B6350 Cornhill to Kelso road. Being flat and straight, the road encourages motorists to speed along, barely noticing that they have passed through a village at all. Looking ahead along the road, the prospect is indeed a little dull. This is one of the very few places along Tweed that is flat. The view south into Northumberland or north across the river into Berwickshire is rather more pleasant. Hills and woods remind the traveller that he is progressing along a valley. The hill that rises immediately behind Wark is called Mount Pleasant, but the hill just upstream has a much more evocative name – Gallows Hill. Just at the Kelso end of Wark stand the barely recognizable remains of Wark Castle. A comparison with Norham would be easier if more of its once-mighty walls and tower had survived. Sadly, what did remain – after four and a half centuries of continually tested garrison – was demolished, ironically for safety's sake, and incorporated into local buildings and farm walls. The site of the old castle is chilly but mainly because of the cold

February wind that blows across the bleak riverside field on which it stands. An old Northumbrian couplet tells simply of Wark's past:

Auld Wark upon the Tweed
Has been mony a man's dead.

The first castle to be built at Wark was erected on the direct orders of Henry I (1068–1135) in the early twelfth century. It did not have to wait long to have its strength tried. It was besieged in 1138 by David I who eventually withdrew his troops to conduct his more successful siege of Norham. Wark garrison replenished their depleted stores by intercepting the Scottish supplies being brought down to nourish David's men at Norham. So incensed was the king that he returned to blockade Wark. In 1343 Wark again resisted a Scottish siege. The castle was occupied at the time by Joan, Countess of Salisbury. Immediately after the withdrawal of the Scots, Joan sent a request for reinforcements to King Edward III (1312–77) who was close by. The king duly arrived with his guard. It is said that at the celebratory feast to honour the king, Joan somehow lost her garter. The king retrieved the garter and put it on his own bestockinged leg, rebuking those of his company who found mirth in the situation with the words 'Honi soit qui mal y pense' (roughly, 'Shame on you!'). The founding of the Order of the Garter is also claimed by Windsor Castle, whose historians give it a later date.

Wark was destroyed in 1399 but rebuilt with even greater strength. The Scots under Sir Robert Ogle held Wark for a very brief period in 1419. They infiltrated the castle by way of the sewers that ran straight into Tweed. Once inside, ladders were thrown over the walls and the rest of their troops entered and quickly took the castle. Unfortunately the Scots failed to pull the ladders back up. As the Scots rejoiced in their victory, the English used the conveniently placed ladders to retake the castle. The short-lived Scots garrison were all beheaded and their bodies thrown over the outer wall. Weakened by the cruel and hard winter of 1460, the English occupants of Wark were routed by the Scots and the castle was again destroyed. The English later took what was left and rebuilt the fort more strongly still.

In 1523 the Scots crossed Tweed at Coldstream once more in an attempt to take Wark. This time they were aided by heavy artillery and a contingent of French troops. On the first day they succeeded in breaching the outer wall and on the second day would undoubtedly have been able to penetrate fully and take the castle. However, heavy overnight rain saw the river rising alarmingly and the Scots were forced to withdraw to Coldstream for fear of being cut off.

By the early eighteenth century English military engineers found Wark Castle so decayed as to make it unsafe, even for a makeshift billet, and it was left to the elements to carry out what armies had tried for so long to achieve – the total destruction of Wark. A measure of the importance the castle held for the English, in its first 300 years, is the fact that it was visited by all but two English kings.

A few miles upriver from the small village of Wark is the equally tiny village of Carham. Set a little back from the river, it huddles around the B6350. Carham church, St Cuthbert's, although not of any great age or architectural interest, does occupy a lovely position. Standing to one side and slightly down from the village, it looks as if it has crept as close to the river as it dares. The village itself has a look of one 'improved' in late Victorian times.

If Norham and Wark proved time and again to be places the Scots would rather forget, Carham is certainly not forgotten. No other place can claim to have seen the English beaten so often. In the Dark Ages, before England could be considered one country, Danes inflicted a crushing and bloody defeat on the Saxons. Although few facts and details have survived, it is known that eleven bishops and two counts lost their lives. Another bishop is also claimed to have died of a broken heart on hearing that so many of his brothers had met their Maker in such a violent manner. Most memorable of all, however, is the Battle of Carham in 1018 – Malcolm II's defeat of the Northumbrians, led by their earl-prince, which brought the region as far south as Tweed forever into Scotland. In fact Malcolm did not long hold the area. It was lost to King Canute (d. 1035) or, to give him his proper name, Knud. Although Malcolm bought the lands of Lothian, Merse and Teviotdale back from Canute for one horse, one cow, one serf and a bushel of meal, he also had to recognize the English kings as overlord.

That other great Scottish patriot, William Wallace (c1270–1305), was also at Carham. He did not do battle with the English there, but camped his troops on a hill just outside. Possibly he thought an association with such a place would be a good omen. Wallace's camp site is still known as Wallace's Hill. The year 1370 saw the last defeat of the English by the Scots at Carham.

Almost directly across the river from Carham lie the few houses and couple of farm buildings that form Birgham. Birgham is set 150 ft (50 m) above and back from the river. It really is so tiny as to be missable in the proverbial blinking of an eye. Yet there can be no smaller place that has played a greater role in the destiny of two countries. It was the site of a famous conference between King William the Lion (1143–1214) and the Bishop of Durham concerning the attempt by the English Church to impose its supremacy upon

Scotland. More importantly, in the following century, it was at a parliament held at Birgham that the political fate of Scotland was sealed. On the death of Alexander III in 1286, the only legitimate heir to the Scottish throne was his granddaughter, Margaret, Maid of Norway (c1282–90). In 1288, with Margaret still in Norway, her great-uncle Edward I proposed a marriage between her and his son, later to be Edward II (1284–1327). This marriage could effectively have brought Scotland into Edward I's hands as Margaret's dowry. Although certain of the Scottish nobles opposed the union – notably Bruce and Balliol who themselves were attempting to claim the throne – enough of them agreed to it. In 1289 the Treaty of Salisbury was signed between England, Scotland and Norway. The treaty was ratified by the Parliament of Birgham in March 1290. This gave the governorship of Scotland over to Edward. In July of the same year a further treaty was delivered from Birgham, guaranteeing the independence of Scottish rights and laws. However, the marriage was never to take place. The thirteen-year-old Margaret succumbed to a childhood ailment and died on her way from Norway without ever having set foot on Scottish soil. The conditions agreed at Birgham allowed Edward the power he later used to appoint Balliol his king of Scotland; this effectively started the 300 years of Anglo-Scottish wars.

Half a mile upriver from Birgham and Carham, the banks of Tweed are Scottish, north and south. The Border river is now a Scottish river.

Fishing

Those who fish are optimists. The nature of their sport demands it of them. River conditions are bad, no fresh fish reported, the barometer falling and heavy rain clouds gathering. Undaunted, the Rod will arrive on the river's bank at the appointed time and will assemble and check tackle, keen to start fishing, quite confident that the odd fresh fish must be about. When the rain does start, the Rod will be convinced that it can only improve things – 'a drop of water might be just what's needed'. Driving home fishless at the end of a cold, wet day, the same optimism will create an absolutely positive certainty that conditions will be ideal tomorrow. It is with this same mental approach to their sport that Rods are quite happy to describe the start of Tweed's fishing season on the first of February as 'spring fishing'. It is a month for which some of the worst weather of the year is reserved – ice, snow, driving rain and winds that can slice through the warmest of clothes. But with the first good run of fish, nature's new year has begun.

The term 'spring fish' refers not so much to the months in which they return to the river; some will start appearing as early as late November. Spring fish are those fish that are destined to spend six to ten months in freshwater before spawning. They are highly prized by Rods and gourmets alike because of their superb condition – 'firm of flesh and silver of flank'. Unlike the 'autumn fish', which return with urgency to spawn, their bellies swelled with the eggs or melt of the next generation, springers are virtually solid muscle. Although they tend to have a lower average weight than their autumn counterparts, they are, pound for pound, a greater test for the Rod. Spring fish are undoubtedly the best quality fish of the season. However, the difficulty of catching them, and the conditions in which they are caught, also play a part in exalting them above fish taken at other times of the year. A fisherman's idea of hell would be to spend eternity fishing a river that yielded a 25-pound (12 kg) salmon with every cast.

There are conditions that do prevent even the keenest Rod from fishing – Tweed 6 ft (2 m) above its summer level, swollen by continual rain and running the colour of Brown Windsor soup, and severe ice freezing the river either partially or completely. Grue (thick layers of snow held in suspension and floating down the river) can act as a pontoon, holding the fly or bait and preventing it from getting down into the water. These, albeit frequent, conditions aside, February will find a full complement of Rods on the early spring section of river.

At the start of the year the fish are much more selective about the water conditions on which they are prepared to run. In clear, warmer water of 35–40°F (2–4°C) with a reasonable flow, fish will travel up as far as Kelso Cauld. Cold, low or high water and they are reluctant to come much above the lower tidal stretches. Whatever the conditions, it is the lower river that holds out the best hope of a springer.

The quality of rod fishing in the river from Berwick to Carham varies greatly. The upper beats – Birgham, Carham, Wark Lees and Lennel – probably offer the best spring fishing on Tweed, whereas the tidal water at the very bottom of the river is unfished and unfishable.

Five or six years ago, it would have been a lot easier to list the good, bad and indifferent beats on the lower Tweed. Commercial net fishermen and rod fishermen do not mix. Until the mid-1980s there were upwards of twenty-five netting stations, running from the estuary to Tillmouth. In 1986/7, with the commercial viability of their operations in decline, many of the net operators sold their leases to the Atlantic Salmon Conservation Trust. This charitable body bought off all but five of Tweed's salmon fisheries, thus hopefully increasing the stock of fish in the river. Of those that remain, two are operated only part-time – Norham and Paxton – and the remaining three full-time stations are well downriver, in the much more tidal stretch.

The netting method used has remained the same for hundreds of years. A long net with floats on its top edge and weights (traditionally cobbles) on the bottom, is fixed to one bank. A boat is initially rowed across the river, paying out the net as it goes; later, it is rowed back to the home bank, where a team of men draw in the net and remove their haul. This is the only permitted method, and its success depends on the river bed being free of large obstacles. The netsmen are intercepting travelling fish, whereas rod fishermen are trying for resting fish. Fish rest in what are known as *lies* – large rocks and boulders behind and beside which salmon can rest out of the main river current. Without natural lies, fish will travel through and not rest in bare pools. Over the years, netsmen have quite legitimately stripped the riverbed around their station of lies. Now, with the removal of the nets, lies are being reintroduced to many of the net-free fisheries. The effect of these changes has been to increase the quality of rod fishing in many of the lower beats.

In the cold water of early spring salmon travel and lie in the deeper parts of the river. Unlike summer fish, they are less inclined to come up to take a fly or bait close to the surface. The fisherman has to ensure, therefore, that his tackle will get the lure down to the lying fish. For the first fourteen days of the season, the only legally permitted method is fly fishing. After the fourteenth – the old start of the netting season (although in practice netting does not nowadays begin until 6 April) – spinning baits and worms may be employed. Although flies used at this time of year have some weight, often being made on a brass or heavy-gauge wire body, it is the density of the flyline that 'sinks' the lure. Spinning baits are metal bodies of different shapes and sizes, to which a treble hook is attached. When drawn through the water either by the current or by the fisherman, they spin or wobble, enticing the fish to take them. Because of the size of Tweed in these lower reaches, boats are frequently used. The boatman is able to put his Rod over all the known lies on the beat. Some Rods do wade, but as well as being exceptionally cold at this time of year, the width of the river does not allow the water to be covered comprehensively.

Once a fish is hooked, the Rod is keen to see if it is a fresh salmon. At this time of year it is just as likely to be a kelt returning to sea. If it is a kelt, she will be safely landed and immediately returned to continue her journey. If it proves to be a fresh fish, the Rod, of course, will delight in the knowledge that he has caught that most highly prized of fish – a Tweed springer.

Paxton House (*left*)

Designed by Robert Adam and built in 1758, Paxton House is a particularly fine example of the neoclassical style favoured at the time. The interior is equally elegant.

Norham Castle (*right*)

The massive remains of the once-monumental keep of one of the strongest forts ever built.

Norham and Ladykirk Bridge (*overleaf*)

Spanning the broad, slow lower river, the bridge replaced the ford which at times of war was so often used to cross invading or retreating armies.

Ladykirk (*left*)

The few souls who inhabit the village are well served by the splendid church, which was built at the beginning of the sixteenth century on the instructions of James IV of Scotland.

Twizel Bridge and castle (*right*)

The simple stone bridge that crosses the River Till at Twizel played a crucial part in Scotland's defeat at the Battle of Flodden in 1513.

Flodden monument (*left*)

The monument, which was erected at the beginning of this century, commemorates the dead of both nations who fell at Flodden Field.

Flodden Field (*right*)

Winter wheat grows on the scene of what was, in September 1513, the battle that effectively ended Scotland's hopes of achieving independence.

Coldstream Bridge (*left*)

The toll house at the Scottish end of the solidly built five-span bridge over the Coldstream Cauld (weir) was used for irregular marriages until the middle of the nineteenth century.

Coldstream (*right*)

Perched perilously close to the river and to English soil, this small but handsome town suffered from the incursions of the armies of both nations.

The Hirsel (*left*)

The imposing home of Lord Home of the Hirsel is a fitting residence for a family that had to fight from a castle to maintain its position in the Borders but, with the Act of Union and the coming of peace, was able to adapt to the changed circumstances and achieve prosperity through farming.

Wark Castle (*right*)

Although now barely visible, the second, larger mound still bears traces of the once mighty and much fought over Wark Castle.

Birgham (*left*)

The few houses and farms that today form the village of Birgham belie the fact that, seven centuries ago, it was host to parliaments that sealed the fate of Scotland.

Carham Church (*right*)

The last of Tweed's English churches, St Cuthbert's Church stands on a cold, exposed site. Although it was the scene of many Scottish victories, Carham soil remains English.

LATE SPRING

Eden Hall to Rutherford Weir

Kelso Abbey (1) • Roxburgh Castle (2) • Floors Castle (3) • Jedburgh Abbey (4)
The Trows (5) • Makerstoun House (6) • Roman Burial Mound (7)
Smailholm Tower (8) • Hume Castle (9)

Kelso

John Rennie's five-arched bridge was built in 1803. Beyond it may be seen the spires of Kelso's churches and the tower of the old abbey.

FROM THE POINT AT WHICH TWEED BECOMES A SCOTTISH river, it is 12 mi (19 km) to the weir at Rutherford. Spring is a fine time to appreciate the unique qualities of this stretch of river. One of the many beauties of Tweed is that throughout its long course the river and the surrounding country change so much and so subtly. None of the changes is sudden.

Driving along the A699 from Kelso to St Boswells, one becomes aware of higher land coming closer to the river and more woodland appearing both beside and away from the water. Gradually the open farming country of the lower river has become farmed parkland.

Were it not that the landscape is so extensive, it would be easy to believe that it was the work of Lancelot (Capability) Brown himself. Certainly all the components of his garden design genius are present – hills, woods, water, ruins and neoclassical houses. Indeed, some of the houses are contemporary with Brown and much of the tree plantation dates from the same period. However, the ruins are not follies and the hills and river represent the work of God rather than the hand of Man. With the warmer weather of spring, trees in full bud, sheep and lambs grazing on new-grown pasture, wide blue skies and the river running deep and clear, this is a place of Arcadian beauty.

This section of Tweed and its valley is civilized and well proportioned. Possibly it is the lack of dramatically large features in the landscape that encouraged the gentrification of the area in the eighteenth century. There are still at least eight grand houses along this relatively short section. As well as the few small villages to be found along its length, the spring river has – or at least had – two very important towns. Kelso, according to Scott, is the most beautiful, if not necessarily the most romantic, town in Scotland. But Roxburgh, the other great town, no longer exists. With the exception of the stumpy, barely recognizable remains of its castle, all that is left of what was once the largest and most influential royal town in Scotland is its memory.

Starting just above Carham, the spring section of river continues upstream as a border, but not a national one. For the first mile of its course it serves as the demarcation line of the counties of Berwickshire to the north and Roxburghshire to the south. The county line leaves the river to travel northward shortly before Tweed is joined by Eden Water – an attractive little stream whose name sets the scene for the delights to come.

Eden Water passes through the village of Ednam a few miles before it enters Tweed. Ednam is a contraction of its old name Edenham. Never a place of any size, it does nevertheless have a rather interesting past. Early in the twelfth century there was a monastic house at Ednam. Its hospital, which was well established by the fourteenth century, must have been kept busy by the warring armies constantly present in the area at the time. In 1715, supporters of James Stuart, the Old Pretender (1688–1766), gathered on Ednam bridge rallying to an already lost cause in a final echo of past battles.

As eighteenth-century bourgeois prosperity progressed, Ednam was also able to claim three noteworthy sons. It was William Dawson, a local farmer and agriculturist, who introduced the first commercially successful system for turnip-growing to Scotland. The humble 'neep' may not seem such a noteworthy crop, but since its introduction it has proved an invaluable winter feed for sheep. The Manse at Ednam was the birthplace of James Thomson (1700–48). Although now little remembered, save for his writing of the ode 'Rule Britannia', he was to poetry what Scott was to the novel. His greatest work, *The Seasons*, was monumental in extent – nearly 4000 lines in length. For over a hundred years after his death he was considered to be the poet *par excellence*, not just by the *literati* but by the wider public in general. When Samuel Taylor Coleridge (1772–1834) found a rather scruffy copy of *The Seasons* in an inn he remarked 'That is fame!' Robert Burns (1759–96) wrote an 'Address to the Bard of Ednam'. In 1820 an obelisk was erected in Ednam to honour Thomson. Scott himself took a leading part in this tribute. The influence of Thomson's work was not confined to Britain – in France such writers as Montesquieu, Voltaire and Rousseau, and in Spain, Melendez Valdes, all praised and found inspiration in Thomson's works. Henry Francis Lyte (1793–1847), born in Ednam, was a most prolific writer of hymns. Two of the best known and most often sung of his works are 'Praise my soul, the King of Heaven' and 'Abide with me'.

A little up from Eden Mouth, Tweed passes around a small wooded island and tumbles over the cauld at Banff Mill. Beyond the weirs, the river describes a long, lazy S reminiscent of Hogarth's 'line of elegance'. It is as the river begins to straighten out that the houses and parks of the area really begin. Opposite the small village of Sprouston, which stands on the south bank, is Hendersyde Park. Separated from the river by the A698 Coldstream to Kelso road, Hendersyde is a large, well-planted estate. Beautifully positioned on the gentle slopes of Tan Law, the three houses on the estate – Hendersyde, Springhall and Sharpitlaw House – all command splendid views over Tweed to the steadily rising Roxburghshire countryside beyond. From Sharpitlaw Anna, a rather large, well-wooded island that stands close to the north bank, it is a short distance upriver to Kelso.

Roxburgh and Kelso

Kelso fits into the inside of a large bend on the north bank of the river. On the south bank is Maxwellheugh, a small town whose streets run steeply down to the river, appearing almost to push visitors over the bridge and into Kelso. It is at Kelso that Tweed is joined by the River Teviot. Flowing through Hawick and past Jedburgh, Teviot is one of Tweed's largest and most important tributaries, and it has a marked effect on the size and appearance of the main river; above the confluence of the two rivers, Tweed becomes narrower — narrow in a relative sense, for its breadth is still substantial — and altogether brighter and livelier. At times, however, the contrast is greatly exaggerated. When Teviot's watershed receives noticeably more rain than that of upper Tweed, the river downstream of Kelso can dwarf its upstream parent.

Just before Teviot enters Tweed, and also on the south bank, is Springwood Park. The Springwood estate, surrounded on two sides by woods and bounded on the other two by the Teviot, was for a long time the seat of a branch of the ancient Douglas family, the Douglases of Springwood. The land between Tweed's south bank and Teviot's north bank is the site of the long-vanished town of Roxburgh.

The extinct city of Roxburgh and the thriving town of Kelso both have violent and troubled pasts, sharing a common history with the towns and villages of the lower river. They were all too familiar with wars, sieges and wanton destruction – as attested by the final, total obliteration of Roxburgh. But for their inhabitants, life offered more than just the shedding of blood and the holding of land.

In 1460 Roxburgh ceased to exist. This date is well known and well documented. Quite when Roxburgh came into being, however, is uncertain. It was always said to be the oldest town in the Borders. Certainly there was a castle and a well-established settlement there by the early twelfth century. Looking at a map of the area, it is easy to see why Roxburgh was founded. The triangular piece of land between Teviot and Tweed is naturally defended on two of its three sides by flowing water. Access to Tweed's north bank is less of a problem across the narrower river above the confluence than across the broader stream below. And almost at the apex of the triangle a mound of land affords the perfect site for a castle. Added to the location's obvious advantages of accessibility and defence, the river offered a water supply and water power as well as fish. The surrounding land was of excellent agricultural quality and the local woods provided both fuel and an abundance of game.

Until 1128 Roxburgh would have had an uninterrupted view north across Tweed and the country beyond. In 1113 David I had brought a colony of Benedictine monks over to Scotland from France. They were first settled at Selkirk on the banks of Ettrick Water. For brothers accustomed to the mild climate of Picardy, the bitter winds and isolation of Selkirk proved more of a test of their bodies than their spirits could endure. So in 1126 they were moved to the more salubrious and sociable area of Roxburgh. Two years later, on 3 May, David granted them a charter to etablish an abbey on Tweed's north bank opposite Roxburgh. The name of the place was given as Kalchu. Very probably this is a descriptive name derived from the chalk cliff or outcrop which is to be found there. By 1176 the then abbot, John, was spelling the name as we do today – Kelso.

Although the development of Roxburgh and Kelso was inextricably linked, their identities always remained quite separate, not simply because they were divided by Tweed but because each served a different purpose – Roxburgh, matters defensive and secular, and Kelso, spiritual and religious needs. Of David's four royal boroughs – Stirling, Berwick, Roxburgh and Edinburgh – Roxburgh was without a doubt his favoured residence. It was, in effect, the capital of the now united Scotland. The widsom of siting the most important city in the realm on the Border may seem a little dubious. However, had David's territorial ambitions for Northumberland and Cumberland been wholly realized, Roxburgh would have had a buffer zone of almost 100 miles (160 km) between itself and England.

Religion and culture

David I is remembered more for his piety than for his military successes or even for his attempt to forge one nation from the disparate remnants of the clannish Pictish tribes that he had inherited. Of the great Border abbeys founded by David – Melrose, Kelso, Dryburgh and Jedburgh – it was obvious that Kelso, being closest to the seat of power, would become the richest and most influential. The first-ever national assembly of Scottish clergy was held at Roxburgh in 1126. This assembly and the visit of a papal legate the previous year were all part of David's attempts to remove the Scottish Church from the influence of the See of York. The separation was achieved two years after the assembly when the Archbishop of York consecrated Robert, Bishop of St Andrews 'for the love of God and of King David'. The leadership of the Scottish Church, which was faithful to Rome, was reluctantly passed from St Andrews to Kelso in 1165. Pope Alexander III granted the privilege of the Mitre to the Abbot of Kelso, thus allowing him to recognize no supremacy other than that of Rome.

The building of the great Abbey of Kelso took eighty-four years to complete. Dedicated to the Blessed Virgin and St John the Evangelist, it was to be a massive structure in the late Norman style. Its cruciform groundplan was unusual; the west end of the cross forming the nave made it shorter than the chancel. The nave and transepts extended barely 23 ft (7 m) from the central tower. The huge tower, some of which still remains, can easily be mistaken, when viewed from a distance, for the tower of a Norman castle.

The wealth of the abbey was prodigious. It received endowments from both landowners and the Crown and enjoyed the exclusive right to mill corn; all mills not owned by the church had to pay a licence fee. The caulds or weirs formed in Tweed to drive the mills were not the strong stoneworks of today. They were constructed of wood and needed to be replaced after each heavy flood. The timber to replace them came from Jed Forest, as did the wood fuel for both Kelso and Roxburgh. With sole rights to the salt beds on the Forth and Solway Firths, the abbey held and sold that most valuable of commodities – salt. The cutting and drying of peat and turf was controlled by the church, which also owned extensive fishings along Tweed and the Teviot. Moreover, tithes from huge tracts of land provided additional revenue for the abbot.

King David had spent much of his youth at the court of Henry I, the scholar king. It was there, according to William of Malmesbury (c1080–c1143), that his manners were 'polished from the rust of Scottish barbarity'. That David chose Benedictine monks to be installed first at Roxburgh, then at Kelso, is explained by their tradition of scholarship and study. Cistercian orders were founded in other Border abbeys and their skills in land husbandry greatly benefited the area. David was a man of learning and wished to be associated with other scholarly men. From its earliest years, Kelso had a thriving scriptorium, and Roxburgh, uniquely in Scotland in the twelfth century, had a grammar school.

Kelso and Roxburgh under David I were developed into centres of excellence, culture and civilization to rival any in Europe. Roxburgh was a city of opulence and magnificence, its safety and defence guaranteed by the massive royal castle that dominated the city from its elevated position. The dimensions of the castle site – 400 yds (400 m) by 100 yds (100 m) – made it by far the largest such building in northern Britain. As well as the abbey across the river, Roxburgh had its own church. Being a royal borough, it also held courts of justice. Law was administered by the Sheriff of Roxburgh who had at his disposal the castle keep, which acted as the state prison. The coin of the realm was made at Roxburgh's royal mint. Together with Berwick, Roxburgh was the trading centre for Scotland. Regular markets were supplemented with fairs that encouraged both commercial enterprise and festivities and entertainment.

The rise and fall of Roxburgh

In 1239, Alexander (later to be Alexander II) married Mary de Coni at Roxburgh. This marriage between the royal houses of Scotland and France marked the beginning of Scotland's oldest alliance, aptly called the 'Auld Alliance'. Alexander III was born at Roxburgh Castle. It was after his death in 1286 that Roxburgh went into decline. Over a hundred years earlier, William the Lion had, as a hostage of Henry II, signed Scottish ownership of Edinburgh, Stirling, Roxburgh and Berwick, as well as the Scottish marches and the independent Scottish church, over to English rule. However, Scottish supremacy was restored, or rather sold back to William by Richard Coeur de Lion (1157–99) in 1189. The price paid was 10,000 marks (£100,000), which Richard used to finance his first crusade.

As with the rest of Scotland, Roxburgh fell under English rule following Edward I's invasion in 1290. One of the signatories to the Ragman Roll was le Pastour of Roxburgh. In 1296 Edward celebrated Pentecost at Roxburgh. William Wallace retook the castle and sacked the town but did not hold it for long. Bruce's strongest follower, Douglas, wrested the castle from English hands on Shrove Tuesday 1313. His men, draped in black cloth, crept on all fours under cover of darkness. The single sentry on duty, who mistook them for cattle, was overpowered and the Scots burst into the castle crying 'Douglas! Douglas!' What had been regained by Bruce was given away by Edward Balliol. He handed over Roxburgh and the rest of the Border castles to Edward II in 1334. The Earl of Derby, Edward's lieutenant-general, spent Christmas 1341 at Roxburgh and by all accounts it was a most civilized occasion. Four Scottish knights, including a Douglas, enjoyed feasting, dancing and a jousting tournament. By contrast, the Roxburgh annual fair of 1372 ended in bloodshed and violence. The previous year, a Scottish knight had been murdered and as the English had failed to punish the culprit, the Scots took their revenge. They fell upon the English visitors and slaughtered them to a man.

The city of Roxburgh was built almost entirely of wood. It was therefore quite easy to destroy when assaulting the castle. The final wasting of the town came in 1460 when James II besieged the castle. James was killed by one of his own pieces of artillery, a large Flemish cannon known as 'the lion'. His queen concluded the siege and ordered the stone-by-stone destruction of the castle. While this took place, she had their son crowned James III over Tweed at Kelso Abbey. The English afforded some very temporary repairs to the remains of Roxburgh Castle in 1547, but this was no more than a patching-up with earth and turf.

Just as there is no certain date for the founding of Roxburgh, there are no records of when the stone bridge that linked Roxburgh and Kelso was built. It is only through references to its destruction in 1547 that its very position can be guessed at. It is believed to have crossed from Roxburgh to somewhere close to the present site of Floors Castle. In its time it would have been the only bridge between Berwick and Peebles. The description of the 'Remains of Roxburgh' written by the Roxburghshire poet, physician and linguist John Leyden (1775–1811) at the end of the eighteenth century, is as fresh and accurate now as the day he penned it:

> Roxburgh! how fallen since first in Gothic Pride
> Thy frowning battlements the wars defied,
> Called the bold chief to grace thy blazon's halls,
> And bade the river gird thy solid walls!
> Fallen are thy towers, and, where thy palace stood,
> In gloomy grandeur waves yon hanging wood;
> Crushed are thy halls, save where the peasant sees
> One moss-clad ruin rise between the trees;
> The still green trees whose mournful branches wave
> In solemn cadence o'er the hapless brave.
> Proud castle! fancy still behold thee stand,
> The curb, the guardian of this border land,
> As when the signed flame, that blazed afar,
> And bloody flag proclaimed impending war,
> While in the lion's place the leopard frown'd
> And marshalled armies hemm'd thy bulwarks round.

LEYDEN, *Scenes of Infancy*

Roxburgh Castle (*right*)

Apart from the mound, nothing now remains of Roxburgh Castle, which was dismantled in 1460 on the orders of Mary of Gueldres, widow of James II of Scotland, who was accidentally killed while his army was investing the castle.

War, plague and fire

Kelso's abbey did not asssure the town an easy passage through the years of Border Wars. Although some sanctuary was to be had within the monastery walls, the surrounding town was always vulnerable to invading forces. The abbey itself was finally destroyed, as were all the Border abbeys, by the Earl of Hertford (1500–52), acting for

Kelso Town House (*left*)

Kelso's large and spacious market square is dominated by the Town House, which was built in the early nineteenth century. The surrounding buildings are a little older.

Kelso Abbey (*right*)

Founded in 1128, Kelso Abbey was the largest of the Border abbeys, and although insufficient of the building now stands to give a true indication of its structure and form, the remains are nonetheless imposing.

King Henry VIII, in 1545. The few monks that did remain lasted only another fifteen years before a Protestant mob routed them and wrought further destruction to the building. By 1587, more than 450 years after its founding, it was officially deconsecrated. Its site and lands passed to Sir Robert Ker of Cessford, first Earl of Roxburghe, in 1602. Worship did take place again in the abbey. In 1649 a rough roof was thrown over the transept and it served as a church until 1771.

Despite the ravages of war, Kelso managed to survive. With the coming of peace at the start of the seventeenth century, Kelso was able to expand and develop its role as an agricultural centre and market town. The demise of Roxburgh had naturally boosted the trade handled by Kelso. Centuries of successful commerce, often in the face of adversity, had fostered an entrepreneurial spirit that promised to serve the townsfolk well in the future.

The possibility of cross-Border war had faded with the accession of James VI. However, Kelso was to see further troubles, both man-made and natural. In 1637, plague – the Black Death – visited the Borders, striking Kelso with its indiscriminate misery. Two years later, General Leslie brought potential disaster to the area by making Kelso the headquarters of his Covenanters' army, raised against Charles I (1600–49) and his ministers, Laud and Strafford. On this occasion, Kelso survived relatively unscathed. It was not so lucky in 1644 when plague broke out again in the town. As well as its human victims, it claimed the town itself. A year after the calamity, a plague house was being 'cleansed' by fire. The fire became an inferno and the whole town was burnt down. Rebuilding work started immediately and trade was soon re-established. However, the timber construction of its buildings and the lack of an effective fire service left Kelso, as all other towns at that time, vulnerable. Forty years later a fire that began in a malt kiln destroyed the new town within six hours.

The Jacobite rebellions of 1715 and 1745 drew most of their support from the Highland clans. The Lowlanders and Borderers, though sympathetic to the movement, were content to sit tight and await developments. In Kelso's town square, on 24 October 1715, the Old Pretender was proclaimed James VIII of Scotland, James III of England. In 1745 his son, Bonnie Prince Charlie, the Young Pretender (1720–88), rested for a couple of days in Kelso, but despite festivities during his visit, gained little tangible support there.

The market tradition

Being a market town, Kelso welcomed visitors to its sales and fairs. As well as generating revenue, markets were apt to lead to high spirits and rowdiness. Rivalry also existed between the young farm workers and the sons of the growing middle classes who attended Kelso grammar school. In 1716 an attempt was made to curb what was becoming unacceptable behaviour by banning of the playing of football (which dispels the idea that football hooliganism is a new problem).

Eighteenth-century Kelso, however, is rather better remembered for the wave of building, change and gentrification which engulfed the town. Floors Castle was one of the earliest Georgian mansions in the area. What is now the Ednam House Hotel was designed and built by James Nisbet for James Dickson in 1761. Dickson was a local man who had started his working life as a saddler's apprentice. He accidentally broke a lamp one night and started a fire which destroyed a large, and by all accounts ugly, pantwell – the town well – that stood in the town square. Fearing the consequences of the accident, he fled to London where he prospered and amassed great wealth as a naval agent and merchant. The Nisbet House was originally called Havana House, much of Dickson's trade having been with Cuba. He also had the Cross Keys Hotel built which still stands in the square. It was Dickson who reintroduced horse racing to Kelso.

Kelso's town square has a very definite French feel to it. It is large and open, not closed in by its buildings. Most of the present buildings date from after 1790. Prior to that date it was described as being reminiscent of a Flemish town square, smaller and surrounded by tall gabled and thatched houses and shops.

A little over 200 years after the destruction of the original stone bridge, Kelso provided a replacement. The new bridge lasted less than fifty years before being washed away by a freakishly large flood in October 1797. Kelso waited only three years before replacing it. John Rennie's (1781–1821) beautiful five-span bridge, almost 500 ft (150 m) long and 25 ft (7.6 m) wide, was completed in 1803 at a cost of £18,000. So successful was his design that he was able to repeat it for London's original Waterloo Bridge. When Waterloo Bridge was demolished in 1935, two of its lamp standards were brought to Kelso. They now stand at the south end of the bridge. Kelso's fine neoclassical Town House that dominates the square was built in 1816, the cost of its construction being borne by James, Duke of Roxburghe.

Much of Sir Walter Scott's early life was spent in and around Kelso. He was a pupil at the grammar school for a short time in 1783. Among the friends he made there were the Ballantyne brothers, John and James. It was on the presses of the Ballantynes' Tory newspaper, *The Kelso Mail*, that the first edition of Scott's *Minstrelsy of the Scottish Border* was printed in 1802. And it was the collapse of the Ballantynes' Edinburgh printing and publishing house, in which Scott was an investor, that bankrupted him. Assuming their debts, he attempted to pay off all the creditors with the proceeds from the publication of the Waverley novels and all his future works.

Kelso's special markets or fairs date back to charters granted at the time of William the Lion. The twice-yearly hiring fairs continued well into the nineteenth century. They were always said to be the jolliest in Scotland. The trade they generated was, for the local traders, even better than the commercially and socially successful race meetings held at Kelso.

Kelso continues to prosper. Its agricultural markets are, of course, less frequent than they used to be, but those that are held now, at Springwood Park, just across Tweed, are much larger affairs. Kelso is now, as it has been for many centuries, a beautiful town in a magnificent position. First published in 1800, Leyden's *Scenes of Infancy*, from which the description of the ruins of Roxburgh came, also includes a wonderful observation of Kelso:

> Bosomed in woods, where mighty rivers run
> Kelso fair vale expands before the sun;
> Its rising downs in vernal beauty swell,
> And fringed with hazel each flowery dell;
> Green spangled plain to dimpled lawns succeed,
> And Tempe rises on the banks of Tweed.
> Blue o'er the river Kelso's shadow lies,
> And copse-clad isles amid the waters rise;
> Where Tweed her silent way majestic holds,
> Float the thin gales in more transparent folds.
> New Powers of vision on the eye descend,
> As distant mountains from their bases bend
> Lean forward from their seats to count the view
> While melt their softened tints in vivid blue.
> When liquid silver floods the moonlit plain

And lawns and fields and woods of varying hue,
Bring their warm lustre and pearly dew;
While still landscape more than moontide bright,
Glisters with mellow tints of fairy light.

Floors Castle to Makerstoun

Directly across Tweed from the vestigial remains of Roxburgh Castle is Floors Castle, home of the Dukes of Roxburghe. The present building dates from the start of the eighteenth century. A house had stood on the site since at least 1545 but it was in 1718 that Sir John Vanbrugh (1664–1726) designed a plain Georgian mansion. Scott described Floors as:

> the modern mansion at Fleurs, with its terrace, its woods, and its extensive lawn, forms alltogether a Kingdom for Oberon or Titania to dwell in, or any spirit who, before their time, might love scenery, of which the majesty, and even the beauty, impress the mind with a sense of awe, mingled with pleasure.

It must be remembered however that Scott was not writing about the massive neo-gothic pile we see today. This is the work of William Playfair, the London-born but Edinburgh-based architect who was responsible for many of Edinburgh's finest buildings, including the Scottish National Gallery. Playfair was commissioned in the 1840s to alter the Vanburgh house. He added the east and west wings and festooned the complete building with castellated battlements, pepperpot towers and water spouts. The overall effect is a successful transformation from a house for a family 'come up in the world' to a ducal castle. The first Duke received the title Lord Ker of Cessford in 1603 from James VI, whom he had accompanied to London on the occasion of his being crowned James I of England. The family had 'come up' indeed, although the Kers of Cessford had been a strong Border family of farmers and landowners since John Ker founded the line in 1356.

Above Floors, Tweed flows through some of the loveliest country to be found along its whole course. Terraced hills and neat fields of pricelessly productive land are broken by elegantly planted woods. The middle ground is of rich grazing land backed by high, distant hills. A few miles up from Floors Castle, again on the north bank, stands Makerstoun House and, a mile behind that, the tiny village of Makerstoun.

Makerstoun House is the most recently built mansion in the Borders. The old house, completely destroyed by fire a few years ago, had a long history of reconstruction and refashioning. Newly rebuilt to original designs by William Adam, the exterior now appears very much as it did in the eighteenth century, commanding what is perhaps the finest site of any of Tweed's great houses. From the oriel window at the top of the rear of the house, the view is almost perfect. A long sloping lawn, planted with huge specimen beech trees and in spring swathed with daffodils, leads down to Tweed. Across the river a bank of trees is interrupted only by the cone-shaped earthwork of a Roman burial mound; straight ahead and in the distance are the Cheviot Hills, and to the west, the triple peaks of the Eildon Hills.

The village of Makerstoun is little more than a few cottages and houses. The monastic house of Malcarvastun founded in 1165 has long since gone. Although of a very much later date, the village church is attractive, if rather plain, on the outside but has an interesting interior. Its boxed pews for the congregation are overseen by the elevated and separated laird's pew. Very much the norm in the nineteenth century, this arrangement has been replaced with open pews in most churches.

Journeying upstream from Makerstoun to Rutherford, you can see Tweed flowing on through wooded banks and around a couple of wooded islands. A narrower river than that at Carham, its beauty has grown and developed into one of stunning pastoral loveliness.

Fishing

The definition of 'spring' is a matter of individual perception. Although the start of the season may be marked officially by the arrival of 22 March or by the date on which the clocks go forward an hour, the British weather is not known for its adherence to clock or calendar. Fishermen clad in thermal clothing, lashed by near-freezing rain and north-easterly winds, may claim to tell spring from winter, but it is a fine distinction. But for the rest of us, longer, warmer days – gentle breezes and light refreshing rains – are the things of spring. April and May, of course, can bring foul weather, too, but they are months of hope and expectation. Rods fortunate enough to fish on the exclusive and excellent beats of Tweed in late spring cannot fail to be optimistic. Given a reasonable flow of water and a supply of fresh fish, there are halcyon days to be had between Birgham and Rutherford, and always the anticipation of a large silvery salmon with the next cast.

The fish, too, respond to changes in temperature. Cold water slows salmon down and causes them to lie low in the water. They are reluctant to move far to intercept a fly or bait. Warmer air and hence warmer water encourage the fish to travel farther and faster.

The flows of other great east-coast salmon rivers to the north may continue to be augmented by melting snow from their catchments well into May. Tweed's flow, however, relies on rain alone for all but the hardest months. This allows the Rods to set aside heavier sinking flylines and weighty flies quite early in the season. Although they may not put their heavy tackle away until the warm months of summer, they can already bring lighter slow-sinking lines and even floating lines into use. For the fly fisherman, lower density lines are much less taxing and more satisfying to cast.

Rods who prefer spinning baits respond to warmer water by changing the size and weight of their lures. Cold water will demand baits of up to 1 oz (28 g), with the possible addition of some extra weight affixed further up the line. With warmer water of around 50°F (10°C) and above, the baits will halve in size and carry additional weight for use in only the heaviest and deepest water. The other bait allowed at this time of year is the worm, often euphemistically known as the 'garden fly', fished with a spinning rod and reel, the weights and hooks carrying the worm or worms attached to the end of the line. The bait is cast in much the same way as with the spinning bait, but the worms are allowed to sink and trundle along the bottom of the river.

The beats of this stretch of Tweed – Birgham Dub, Sprouston, Hendersyde, Junction, Floors, Makerstoun and Rutherford – are arguably the finest on the river. They fish well from the start of the season and steadily improve, diminishing only for a short hiatus in summer. The Junction Pool on Junction Water at Kelso is the most productive few hundred yards of water on Tweed, and possibly in Europe. As its name implies, it is at a junction – that of Tweed and Teviot. The Teviot is itself a renowned salmon river. Salmon intending to ascend the Teviot will wait at the junction for suitable water before continuing their journey; those bound for Tweed likewise pause at the junction prior to negotiating the formidable Kelso weir. Although by no means the most attractive pool on Tweed – the busy A699 runs parallel to it – it offers exceptional sport to fishermen and the opportunity for passers-by to view the fascinating battle between Rod and fish. Even above the confluence with the Teviot, Tweed is still a mighty river. Boats, with their attendant boatmen, are essential for covering the water.

As the sea is left increasingly far behind and the river gradually narrows, Rods, whether in shirtsleeves or wrapped up warmly against a late chill, are more often to be seen wading and fishing from the bank. This section of Tweed, flowing through the Arcadian beauty of its valley, is guaranteed to delight and excite all who fish it.

The Lairds Cast

Fast fast, we have him fast —
A prime one by the gleam!
In the auld Lairds shadowy cast
Above the Elshie stream:
'Tis a salmon plump and strong
Newly from the flowing brine
Nearly run Nearly run — a right thundering one —
Tell me line.

Away he darts away
Across the gleaming Tweed
Nor art nor arm can stay
The glorious creature's speed
From our reel the swift line flies
As he feels the galling sear
And in vain, all in vain shakes his lengthening chain
from afar.

To shore, slow draw to shore
The light boat edges in,
While moves the cautious oar
Like some sea-prowlers fin
In the creeks of an Indian Isle;
Now the flowers bank we've gain'd
And in hand, firm in hand, with our labouring wand
Hold him chain'd.

See, see in fierce dispair
He seeks by frantic spring
To snap the yielding hair
To fly the madd'ning string.
In vain, all in vain, his headlong plunge!
For the fatal die is cast.
O'er his eyelids soon death's glimmering swoon
Shall have pass'd.

With quick revolving hand
The good line home we wind,
While obedient to our wand
The worn fish floats behind;
And the bright pebbled edge as he nears,
With oor gaff-hook we check his retreat,
And see here he lies – a weltering prize
At our feet.

COLLECTED BY THOMAS TOD STODDART
An Angler's Rambles, 1866

A proud moment

Young Ben Gwynne just about manages to show off the 10-lb hen fish he has caught in the Doors Pool of lower Makerstoun Water.

Ednam House Hotel (*left*)

Now greatly enlarged, the original Havana House, which was built for merchant James Dickson in 1761, can still be seen as the central portion of the present building.

Ednam House: interior
(*right*)

Above the ornate fireplace hangs a portrait of James Dickson. The comfortable chairs, open fire, old wood and fishing rods contribute to the club-like atmosphere of the hotel and draw Rods to fish Tweed.

Floors Wall (*left*)

Part of the huge wall that encloses the planted parklands of Floors Castle. The wall was built during the Napoleonic Wars of the early nineteenth century by French prisoners of war.

Floors Castle (*right*)

The seat of the Dukes of Roxburghe, the original Adam building was enlarged and extended by William Playfair in the nineteenth century. It is said to be the largest inhabited house in Scotland.

Roman burial mound (*left*)

The mound, which is formed of alluvial shale, is believed to date from Roman times. Protected on one side by water, it would have served as either a fort or a look-out station.

The Trows (*right*)

Whether 'The Trows' were formed by demonic intervention or simply by the power of water flowing between outcrops of rock, Tweed is here forced through a channel that is deeper than it is wide.

Makerstoun House (*left*)

Occupying a magnificent site, which for more than eight centuries has been used by Border families, the present building is an award-winning reconstruction of an earlier Makerstoun House.

Makerstoun House: the dining room (*right*)

Much of the original Peel tower remains within the elegant Adam interior. The dining room on the ground floor, with its simple vaulted ceiling and wall up to 4 yards (4 m) thick, would have been used to shelter animals.

Hume Castle (*left*)

An eighteenth-century folly now occupies the site where, in former times, stood the mighty and much assaulted seat of the Hume (now Home) family. From the top of the castle a clear view could be had of the Lammermuir Hills to the north, the Cheviots to the south, the sea to the east and Tweed to the west.

Smailholm Tower (*right*)

Standing like a sentinel on a bleak and desolate outcrop of rock amid fertile farmland, Smailholm Tower is still evocative of the Border Wars, so vividly portrayed by Sir Walter Scott, who spent his childhood in the shadow of Smailholm at Sandyknowe Farm.

HIGH SUMMER

Little Dean Tower to Ettrickfoot

*Mellerstain House (1) • Rutherford Lodge (2) • Jedburgh Abbey (3)
Dryburgh Abbey (4) • Bemersyde House (5) • Scott's View (6)
Leaderfoot Bridges (7) • Melrose Abbey (8) • Abbotsford (9) • Boleside (10)*

Rutherford Lodge

This civilized, somewhat understated house stands in enviably close proximity to Tweed. Nothing now remains of the mill that was once served by the cauld at Rutherford.

H ERE, IN THE SUMMER SEASON, TWEED CAN BE SEEN AT ITS most romantic – and indeed its most Romantic; fashioned, as it seems, from the stories of Walter Scott as illustrated by J. M. W. Turner. Its landscape is inspiring, beautiful and possessed of grandeur, yet never intimidating or frightening. Where its history is bloody, the blood was shed sufficiently long ago for morbid passion to have drained from it. Myths and legends have been woven into the hills and the valley, enriching historical fact and giving colour to the reality of the landscape.

The rectangular fields of the lower river now give way to the approaching higher ground. Grazing sheep and cattle replace the tidy rows of crops. The increasing number of trees, in full leaf at this time of year, cast shadows and dappled light on the lower, clearer water. The river still retains its familiar long, lazy glides and pools, but is now more frequently broken and hurried as it travels over a rockier bed.

The longer, warmer days of summer, more suited to thinking and dreaming than to arduous labour, show this middle section of Tweed, upstream from Rutherford to Boleside Water, at its glorious best.

The river starts its winding route just below Rutherford Cauld, overlooked from the south bank by the attractively planted grounds of Rutherford Lodge. The weir has been substantially breached. This breach acts as a fish ladder, allowing salmon to make their way upriver in any height of water. On the steep wooded south bank running down to Mertoun Water are the remains of Little Dean Castle with its unusual semi-circular tower, one of the many Peel towers along the length of Tweed. The tower marks the start of the wide loop of river that sweeps around the substantial Mertoun House, home of the Duke of Sutherland, and straightens as it flows under the fine Mertoun Bridge, which, like Kelso's bridge, was designed by Rennie. The small market town of St Boswells on the south bank takes its name from Saint Boisil, the Abbot of Old Melrose Abbey who, in the seventh century, welcomed Cuthbert into his house.

From St Boswells the river turns again and on the inside of this bend, surrounded by specimen trees of yew, cedar and beech, stand the remains of Dryburgh Abbey. Although in ruins, enough of the structure is preserved to give a good idea of how large and impressive an edifice the abbey must have been. It was consecrated for use by an Augustinian Order on 11 November 1150 and, having been attacked and rebuilt twice in the fourteenth century, was finally sacked in 1544 during the Reformation in an assault led by Lord Hertford's subordinates, Evans and Layton. Although the abbey has not been used regularly for worship since this last attack, its grounds are still used for burial.

Among the graves are those of Sir Walter Scott and Field Marshal Earl Haig (1861–1928), whose Poppy Day Appeal is a reminder of another 11 November – Armistice Day. Earl Haig, as Laird of Bemersyde, lies beside a long line of his ancestors. Sir Walter Scott's right of sepulchre is not so straightforward. It stems from the marriage in 1542 between George Halliburton and a Miss Haig. Their son was great-grandfather to the wife of Sir Walter Scott's grandfather.

The river now straightens out as it enters its first gorge. Here it passes below Bemersyde, home of the second Earl Haig and 30th Laird of Bemersyde, whose family has played an important role in Borders history since the mid-twelfth century, when the first reference to it is to be found in the person of Petrus del Haga. The road running alongside the river climbs steeply at this point until it reaches Scott's View. The view afforded from this point, 300 ft (90 m) above a huge loop in the river at Bemersyde, is as complete a picture of Borders country and history as can be seen anywhere – the river winding below the perilously steep and wooded north bank; to the south and west the site of the granary of the Old Melrose Abbey, the three peaks of the Eildon Hills, the town and Abbey of Melrose, Ettrick Forest and, in the distance, the hills where Tweed is born.

Leader Water runs into Tweed beyond Scott's View and opposite Ravens Wood. Three bridges cross the river above Leaderfoot and their different styles accurately reflect the aspirations of their times. The first, a concrete and steel construction of the twentieth century, has no merit other than carrying the four lanes of the A68 trunk road efficiently from one side of the river to the other. Next is Newstead Bridge, a three-arched, buttressed road bridge of sandstone built in the seventeenth century. The boat-shaped piers and symmetrical arches are decorated with round niches and carvings, giving it an aesthetically pleasing and reassuringly strong appearance. The third bridge is a wondrous Victorian railway viaduct. Now disused, it once carried the North British Railway's 'Waverley Line' running between Edinburgh and Hawick. Looking like a piece of fine fretwork, its long slim pillars of local rusticated brick-red sandstone elegantly span the valley.

Melrose Abbey

Over the next 3 mi (5 km), the river runs through a narrow plain. On the south bank, and masked by a small plantation, is the old, sleepy village of Newstead, followed shortly by Melrose, the first town of any size since Kelso. Melrose occupies the low ground between the Eildon Hills and the river. The best-known landmark in this ancient and attractive market town is its abbey. The Cistercian monks from Rievaulx Abbey in Yorkshire, who occupied Melrose Abbey from 1136, are credited with the introduction of sheep farming, which proved to be of crucial economic importance to the area. What remains of the abbey dates largely from its rebuilding in 1325 by a French architect, Jean Moreau. George Meikle Kemp, the previously little-known architect of the extravagantly Gothic Scott Monument in Edinburgh, drew strongly for his 1846 design on the arches of the nave and transept of Melrose Abbey. When he submitted his plans for this monument, he caused some confusion by signing them Jean Moreau, in recognition of the source of his inspiration.

Like Dryburgh, Melrose Abbey was sacked during the Reformation. It later suffered the religious ignominy of having a makeshift wooden roof installed and being used as the town's kirk. Both the heart of Robert Bruce and the body of Alexander II are said to be buried at Melrose Abbey. Beyond Melrose and Darnwick, Tweed can be crossed by way of a charming eighteenth-century bridge. The approach and exit road to the bridge run parallel to the river and slow the motorist for long enough to give a pleasing view of the wooded valley and Lowood House to the north.

The sweep of river that passes the modern industrial estate of Tweedbank on one side and the lower end of the weaving town of Galashiels on the other is fed by Gala Water. Galashiels has long been the centre of the Borders woollen trade and covers the last $2\frac{1}{2}$ mi (4 km) of the Gala Valley. The end of this, thankfully short, industrial section is marked by a very recent and truly graceless road bridge.

A short distance upriver from this bridge, on the south bank, stands Sir Walter Scott's home – Abbotsford. From here to the junction of the Ettrick, Tweed passes through the consistently productive fishing beat of Boleside.

The legacy of literature

'Every valley has its battle and every stream its song.'
Sir Walter Scott, 1830

To attempt to separate Border history, legend and landscape from Scott is akin to unpicking a fine tapestry to assess the colour of the silks. And nowhere is the tapestry more finely woven or the hues more subtle than in the summer section of Tweed.

Born the son of an Edinburgh solicitor in 1771, Walter was a weak and sickly baby.

As six of his brothers and sisters had already died in infancy, it was decided to take him from 'Auld Reekie' to the healthier country air of his grandfather's farm. So it was that as a young child he was delivered into the heart of the borders, to Sandyknowe Farm. Less than 2 mi (3 km) above the river at Mertoun and Rutherford, Sandyknowe Farm stands with its back to Sandyknowe Craigs and in the shadow of Smailholm Tower. The Peel Tower of Smailholm is one of the many sixteenth-century towers built to form a line of communication along Tweed. At the first sign of an invasion or assault, a fire was lit on top of the tower. By day the smoke, and by night the flames, would be sighted by the neighbouring Peel and in this way a call to arms was sent up and down the valley.

Schooled in Kelso, Walter Scott travelled much in the area, and heard tales, poems and songs of battles won and lost, characters and conflicts, fables and facts. When, as a boy, he travelled with his father from Selkirk to Melrose, Mr Scott would have the carriage stopped at a marker stone known as Turn Again Spot. This was where the young man's namesake, Sir Walter Scott (Wicked Wat) of Branxholm, Lord of Buccleuch, stood at bay in August 1526 after being routed by the sixth Earl of Angus at the battle of Melrose Bridge. Angus's force of 300 had been outnumbered two to one by Scott, but received winning help from a squadron of eighty horsemen brought by Lord Home and the Kers of Cessford and Fernyhirst. While standing off at Turn Again Spot, one of Scott's men, named Elliot, slew Ker of Cessford and put an end to their pursuit.

> Where Home and Douglas in the van
> Bore down Buccleuch's retreating clan
> Till gallant Cessford's life-blood dear
> Reeked on dark Elliot's spear.

Turn Again Spot is half-a-mile (800 m) above the river where once stood Clarty Hole (Dirty Hole) Farm. It was renamed Abbotsford when, in 1811, it was bought by Sir Walter.

After Kelso, Scott went back up to Edinburgh where he successfully studied Law and then practised as an advocate. Although parted from the Borders, his fascination with its spirit did not abate. In 1802 he had published in Kelso his three-volume *Minstrelsy of the Scottish Borders* — a collection of ancient and modern ballads, many of which were taken from the oral tradition so strong in this area. With his appointment in 1805 to the office of Sheriff of Selkirkshire he was able, in order to fulfil the requirement to reside in the county, to take up residence at Ashiestiel House. While there, he continued with ever-increasing success and prosperity to publish both prose and poetry.

It was Abbotsford, however, rather than Ashiestel, which will forever be thought of as the home of Sir Walter Scott. Scott bought Abbotsford, then Clarty Hole Farm, in 1811. In a letter to his brother-in-law, Mr Carter, Scott mentioned that he had bought for about £4000 a property of approximately 100 acres (40 ha). 'It is bleak at present and other than its proximity to the river it has little to recommend it', but he thought that by planting trees on half of the acreage he would, given the high price of timber, have a valuable possession in a few years. He added that he intended to build a small cottage here for his summer abode. In fact, for Scott, it had a great deal to recommend it — the river, the very life source of the Borders, the proximity to Turn Again Spot, while along the south-east of the estate, the Huntly Burn ran through the Rhymer's Glen, called after Rhyming or True Thomas (1219–99), poet and prophet. He is best remembered as the author of one of the oldest extant Scottish poems, 'The Romance of Sir Tristren'. His title of True comes from his reputed inability to speak anything but the truth, and hence from the truth of his prophecies. This power was bestowed upon him during his seven-year stay as a servant of the Queen of the Fairies ('gude neighbours') in her kingdom below the Eildon Hills. Although released, he was bound to return when the queen commanded, as she eventually did by sending a hart and a hind to collect Thomas from his village street. He followed the beasts into the forest and has, as yet, not been seen again.

Sir Thomas Lauder, writing of this area in the late nineteenth century, spoke of the 'Scoto-Arcadian district of pastoral poetry and song' and, of course, for our awareness of this, Scott must forever be thanked. He must also be thanked for the immeasurable change he effected on the overall beauty of the area when he planted trees on his newly acquired estate. Until then, this area of the summer river had a very sparse population of trees, but, following his lead, landowners from Rutherford to Boleside began the plantations that today are considered so typical of the area. Since Scott was dead within twenty-one years of buying Abbotsford, he would not, of course, have seen the full effect of this change.

Great as Scott's influence was upon the appearance of his beloved Tweed landscape, it was through his pen that he transformed himself into the greatest cultural figure of his age. This is not the place for a full literary appreciation of Scott's life's work — yet the scale of his reputation among his contemporaries in Europe and beyond cannot be over-emphasized. Suffice it to say that it was as a schoolboy that he first became fascinated by the romantic poetry and literature of fifteenth-century France and Italy, and then by the German revival of Romantic and Gothic poems and tales set in far-off feudal times. Keenly aware of the inexhaustible riches of the Borders' own history, Scott resolved to do for the ancient Borders world what German writers had done for the medieval cities and states of the Rhine. Scott's ballad *The Lay of the Last Minstrel*, published in 1805, followed by *Marmion* in 1808, established him almost overnight as the greatest poet living and as the most potent figure of the growing European Romantic literary movement.

In 1814, Scott published, anonymously, a three-volume historical novel, *Waverley*, which effectively revolutionized European literature. Richly adorned with the fruits of Scott's formidably detailed knowledge of ancient Borders history, tradition and topography, *Waverley* was but the first of an ever-unrolling pageant of novels which convincingly recreated a feudal past of chivalry, violence, adventure, passion and tragedy – all produced at the almost unnatural pace which so perplexed and mystified his contemporaries. Scott's poetry alone had filled twelve volumes in the 1820 edition: his prose novels and tales ran to no fewer than forty-eight volumes in the edition supervised by the author and published between 1829 and 1833, the year following Scott's death. Yet these towering literary monuments formed merely the peak of a mountain of other publications in his roles as critic, historian and literary editor, all achieved in the context of a full public, social and business life. Such was the man who for twenty years looked out from Abbotsford across the river and whose presence remains as enduring a feature of the Borders landscape as Tweed and the Eildon Hills themselves.

In 1826, at the height of his literary powers, Scott's Edinburgh publishers – Constable and Cadell (owned by the Ballantynes of Kelso) – were bankrupted. The intricacies of their business arrangement left Scott assuming their obligations. From then until his death in 1832, Scott worked tirelessly to pay off the accrued debts.

As he had planned, Scott built his small cottage at Abbotsford, but with greater fame came higher aspirations. From 1817 to 1825, Scott supervised a dramatic programme of remodelling and extension, largely to his own designs, which resulted in the Gothic baronial fantasy that is Abbotsford today. John Ruskin considered Scott 'the greatest writer of his age': by contrast, Ruskin's pronouncement that Abbotsford was 'perhaps the most incongruous pile that gentlemanly modernism ever designed' may seem a little cruel, but does reflect the view generally taken of its architecture at the time. The building of Abbotsford, the debts he still bore and the huge output of work he continued to try to produce, all took a grave toll on Scott's health. When, in August 1831, J. M. W. Turner visited Abbotsford, his host was a very sick and weak man. Although it must have been a great effort, Scott conducted Turner around many of the sites the artist had been commissioned to draw, to be used later as illustrations for a series of annotated volumes of Scott's poetic works. Turner was so taken with Scott and all that he had been shown that in 1834, two years after Scott's death, the painter, himself now in poor health, agreed to make the arduous journey north to produce illustrations for the biography of Scott being prepared by his son-in-law, John Lockhart.

The respect and affection generated by Scott was nowhere more obviously displayed than at his funeral. The route from Abbotsford to his final earthly resting place at Dryburgh Abbey was lined, and in places thronged, with people whose genuine grief could not be disguised. It is said that of their own accord, the horses drawing the hearse stopped at the most beautiful spot known as Scott's View.

In his most entertaining and informative book *Days and Nights of Salmon Fishing in the Tweed*, published in 1845, William Scrope speaks of Scott thus: 'Since that time I have seen the cottage of Abbotsford with its rustic porch, lying peacefully on the haugh between the lone hills, and have listened to the wild rush of the Tweed as it hurried beneath it. As time progressed, and as hopes arose, I have seen that cottage converted into a picturesque mansion with every luxury and comfort attached to it, and have partaken of its hospitality; the unproductive hills I have viewed covered with the thriving plantations, and the whole aspect of the country civilized without losing its romantic character. But amidst all these revolutions, I have never perceived any change in the mind of him who made them, "the choice and master-spirit of the age". There he dwelt in the hearts of the people, diffusing life and happiness around him; he made a home beside the Border river in a country and a nation that have derived benefit from his presence, and consequence from his genius. From his chambers he looked out upon the grey ruins of the abbey, and the sun which set in splendour beneath the Eildon Hills. Like that sun, his course has been run; and though disasters came upon him in his career, he went down in unfading glory.'

The Eildon Hills

In all its moods and changes, the river symbolizes and epitomizes the Borders. But there is no worthier emblem of the area than Scott's beloved Eildon Hills. Their three peaks can be seen from many points along almost the entire length of the river. The Romans knew of the Eildons and realized their defensive potential by building a fortification there. The hills are not only said to loom over the Kingdom of the Fairies but are claimed – although not alone in this – to be the site of the burial chamber of King Arthur.

Geologists tell us that the Eildons are ancient volcanic outcrops stranded in an area of softer sandstone. Border tradition has it that they were made by a demon, or imp, in the employ of Michael Scot, a local wizard. That Auld Michael existed is certain. His powers were widely enough known for mention to have been made of him, as Michele Scoto, by Dante in his *Inferno*. Michael, in an attempt to annoy the monks of Melrose whose presence was not conducive to his wizardry, ordered a demon in his service to construct hills to deprive the abbey of sunlight. The demon took a mighty shovel to the Cheviots, each peak being a single shovelful. Returning with the last load, he split half of it, forming Rubershaw Hill; hence the third peak was too low to cast the abbey in its shadow. To escape the wrath of Auld Michael, the demon bent his shovel into a boat and set off downriver. Michael gave chase in one boat, followed by another containing a party of monks and Thomas the Rhymer, who were curious to view the outcome. When the flotilla reached Makerstoun Water, a witch in the guise of a raven reminded Michael that he was powerless in running water. Straight away, he leapt from his boat and ahead of the demon's vessel. Summoning all his power, he tried to dam the river and arrest the demon. Unfortunately, he neglected to remove his foot from the stream. Rather than damming the river, a series of deep channels formed in the rock, concentrating the stream and allowing the demon to escape to the sea, whence he never returned. So narrow were the channels at this point of the river that it was said that at summer levels, a man could leap across the river at 'The Trows'. One poor fellow who tried this at the end of the nineteenth century lost his footing and drowned. The channels were later mechanically widened to prevent a repetition of the sad event.

Just as archaeologists have a prosaic explanation for the formation of the Eildons and the Trows, so scholars describe Michael Scot (1175–1235) not as a wizard but as the leading European intellectual of the early thirteenth century, translator of Arabic and Latin, alchemist, physician and astrologer to the Holy Roman Emperor Frederick II (1194–1250).

Fishing

Of the long season available to fishermen on Tweed, the summer months between mid-May and mid-August would not be everyone's first choice. Those who fish the lower river at this time may encounter reasonable sport with any fresh fish that come in on the tide. But generally, the lower river levels of summer have the effect of holding the fish back. Building up in numbers in the estuary and out at sea, the fish await the rains of late summer to freshen the water and entice them upriver. While off-shore and in the estuary, they are easy prey to the commercial and illegal netsmen who, unlike rod fishermen, are never sad to see a dry summer. Those new fish that choose to run the river in summer will be relying on the showers and subsequent rises in river level to make slow progress upstream. It is unusual at this time to encounter any fish, and particularly clean fish, above the confluence with the Ettrick.

If summer is not generally a very productive time to fish for salmon on Tweed, it is nevertheless a most beautiful time to try. All of the beats along this most pastoral of river sections will hold fish and, given some rain, can promise sport with summer salmon and smaller grilse (fish that have spent only one winter feeding at sea since leaving the river).

The boats rowed and held in place with such deceptive ease by the boatmen in the higher waters of spring and autumn, allowing their Rods to fish the otherwise inaccessible parts of the beat, are not employed during the summer months. This allows the boatmen to take a much-deserved rest from the oars and to see to their other duties – tending to the banks and repairing any riverbed damage caused by the previous winter's storms.

When the whole countryside is refreshed and invigorated by recent summer rain and the river is running above its normal height and slowly falling, Rods can go to the water's side with high hopes of encountering a bright and lively fish. If the weather is settling into a warm, dry spell, then early morning and late evening will be the times to concentrate their efforts. During unsettled conditions, however, no part of the day should be neglected. This is a time of year when stealth really can pay dividends – careful and deep wading, long casts gently placing a smallish fly in likely fish-holding places, there to be held in the water by a floating line. Warmer weather finds fish preferring faster, cooler, more highly-oxygenated water.

The warm, soft light of evening, the splendour of the country in its lush, green coat, and the gentle glide of water breaking and tumbling over half-hidden stones – all combine in such a natural setting to make summer a most delightful time to fish any of the beats between Rutherford Water and Boleside Water.

The summer river

A drift of flowers heralds the arrival of summer on Tweed.

Mellerstain (*left*)

The figure of Mercury, the messenger of the gods, looks down over this beautiful Georgian house, the home of the Earls of Haddington. The wings were built by William Adam, but the central block and the interior are the work of Robert Adam. The house contains one of the finest collections of paintings in Scotland.

Dryburgh Abbey (*right*)

Scattered and fragmented as they are, the ruins of this most beautifully situated abbey still convey much of the grandeur of this imposing house of God.

Scott's Grave (*left*)

It would be hard to find a more peaceful resting place for the soul of Sir Walter Scott than a side chapel of Dryburgh, the Border abbey with which his forebears were most closely associated.

Jedburgh Abbey (*right*)

The fourth of the Border abbeys to be founded by David I, Jedburgh, like Kelso, Melrose and Dryburgh, was founded in the twelfth century. The town of Jedburgh lies on Jed Water, which flows into the Teviot, which, in turn, joins Tweed at Kelso.

Leaderfoot viaduct (*left*)

The sturdy old road bridge contrasts with the delicate railway viaduct, which used to carry trains on the 'Waverley Line' between Edinburgh and Hawick.

Bemersyde (*right*)

The old, central portion of the house, the home of the second Earl Haig, dates mainly from the late sixteenth century. The wings are later additions. The ancient tree in the foreground, said to be over 800 years old, is known as the Hanging Tree.

Melrose Abbey (*left*)

Despite much rebuilding and, sadly, still more destruction, the site still conveys something of the magnificence and tranquillity of the original abbey.

Melrose (*right*)

The market town of Melrose serves the area with its shops and hotels. The cross dates from the sixteenth century, although the column and head are more recent additions.

Abbotsford House (*right*)

A bold example of the style
known as 'Scottish Baronial',
Scott's home overlooks
the river that runs through
the land he loved and
made his own.

The Maxwell-Scotts (*left*)

Mrs Patricia Maxwell-Scott
(right) and her sister, Dame
Jean Maxwell-Scott, are the
great-great-great-
granddaughters of Sir Walter
Scott. They live in and
maintain the family home,
Abbotsford House.

Sir Walter Scott (*left*)

The 1820 bust of the author by Sir Francis Chantrey was described by John Gibson Lockhart, Scott's son-in-law, as 'that bust which alone preserves for posterity the cast of expression most fondly remembered by all who ever mingled in his domestic circle'.

Abbotsford: Scott's study (*right*)

It was in the wood-panelled, book-lined study of Abbotsford House that Scott worked so hard on both his literary works and his legal duties. The gas lamps at Abbotsford were among the first to be installed in any house in the country.

Scott's View (*overleaf*)

This spot, 300 ft (100 m) above the river at Bemersyde, is said to have been Sir Walter Scott's favourite viewpoint. From it are visible the river, the Eildon Hills, Melrose and, in the far distance, the hills that give birth to Tweed.

Boleside (*left*)

The rich greens of summer shade the low water of Tweed as it flows through one of the middle river's most productive fishing beats.

Rod and boatman
(*above right*)

In the lower water boats are often forsaken and Rods wade. Here, worm is fished through the faster, more oxygenated water between and below exposed rocks.

Salmon (*below right*)

At 7 lb and 10 lb neither of these fish is large. However, they are bright, fresh and well-shaped fish, typical of the salmon that can be expected in Tweed at any time between the start of the season and midsummer

EARLY AUTUMN

Sunderland Hall to Mannor Water

New Road Bridge (1) • *Yair Bridge (2)* • *Yair House (3)*
Ashiestiel House (4) • *Elibank Castle (5)* • *Walkerburn Woollen Museum (6)*
Innerleithen Plain (7) Traquair House (8) • *Kailzie Gardens (9)*
Peebles Hydro (10) • *Neidpath Castle (11)* • *Hogg Monument (12)*

Upriver from Ettrick Water

The Tweed valley, upriver
from its confluence with
Ettrick Water, is resplendent
in the shades of autumn.

FOR EARLY AUTUMN, TWEED WILL BE FOLLOWED FOR OVER 20 mi (32 km) from its union with Ettrick Water to its junction with Mannor Water.

This early autumn section of upper Tweed is a land of wood and wool. High hills rise steeply from beside the very river; at best a narrow plain lies between hill and stream. Where access to the plough is possible, some crops are grown, mainly neeps for fodder. Some other root crops and brassicas are raised, but the terrain forbids the economical production of much grain. Trees, however, whether intended as a crop or a renewable resource, are grown in vast numbers in the forests along the whole length of this section of the river.

Those hills not given over to timber production are occupied by sheep. It was not just the rearing of sheep that brought prosperity, especially during the nineteenth century, to these parts. It was mainly the spinning and weaving of wool that sustained the towns of Innerleithen and Peebles and also created Walkerburn, the largest village in the area.

The contours of the land and the presence of the river make this stretch attractive throughout the year. Its true loveliness, however, is fully revealed only in the colours of late September and much of October. From Ettrick to Mannor, a constantly changing weave of colour and tone unfolds and envelops the valley. The designers of the cloth that bears the river's name could never hope to produce a tweed to match the beauty of this place in its autumn clothes. With cold nights, warm days and soft light, upper Tweed is a place of singular charm.

The shepherd of Ettrick

Standing on the new road bridge with your back to the section of summer river, it is difficult, particularly with the traffic on the A7 Carlisle to Edinburgh road roaring behind you, to decide which is Tweed and which is Ettrick. They are of such similar size. The old stone bridge a few hundred yards ahead can be presumed – correctly – to be crossing Tweed, the parent river.

Ettrick is probably best known for two things: its forests and its shepherd. The Ettrick forests were for many centuries the chosen hunting grounds of the Scottish royal family. From David I to Mary, Queen of Scots, the abundance of game and the quality of land provided sport and a diversion from their offices of state. The Ettrick shepherd is, of course, James Hogg (1770–1835), the poet. Born at Ettrick, the second son of a failed farmer, he received, by his own account, less than one year's schooling. At the age of seven he began herding sheep. After eight years of apprenticeship, he was able to offer himself for hire as a qualified shepherd. From 1790 to 1800, he was employed by a Mr Laidlaw of Yarrow. It was the Laidlaws' son William, ten years his junior, who introduced Hogg to a wider field of literature. His rudimentary education had been restricted to the Bible and the catechism. A recitation of Burns's 'Tam-o'Shanter' by a 'half daft man' encouraged Hogg to try to fill the void left by Burns's death in 1796. His first printed work, a song, 'Donald M'Donald', appeared in 1800. The friendship that most shaped Hogg's literary life began in 1802. He and his mother met Scott and supplied him with material for the third volume of his *Border Minstrelsy*. Through Scott, Hogg became acquainted with the Scottish *literati* and the leading figures in the British Romantic movement. One of his finest works, *The Queen's Wake*, was written in 1813 and published in Edinburgh. It was later issued in England by John Murray at the request and suggestion of Byron. Hogg continued to produce strong and imaginative work up until his death in 1835. He was essentially a Romantic. What more romantic a calling for a poet than that of a shepherd? Despite literary success, he never really knew wealth. His disastrous financial dealings as a farmer kept him in near-constant debt. Hogg and Scott are the great Border poets. Scott's claim to this title has been disputed because he was born in Edinburgh. Such a judgement is surely small-minded in the extreme. The truth of what a man is can be seen in his heart, not on his certificate of birth.

Above its union with Ettrick, Tweed is a noticeably narrower river. The lower river is fed only by its largest tributaries. But from Ettrick to its source, Tweed is grateful for the water from all the burns and streams that feed it. The narrowness of the upper river means that bridge-building is less of a feat. The old bridge above Ettrick Foot has been made redundant by the new A7 road bridge that boldly crosses the wider river below. From Ettrick Foot it is only a couple of miles before Tweed is bridged again at Yair. Yair in old Scots is a weir. And it was the weir at Rigged Craig below Yair Bridge that Scott described in the introduction to the second canto of *Marmion*:

> From Yair – which hills so closely bind,
> Scarce can the Tweed his passage find,
> Though much he fret, and chafe, and toil,
> Till all his eddying currents boil.

Just above the bridge on the south bank is the extremely attractive Yair House. An elegant bow-fronted Georgian mansion, it is perfectly sited between the river and Yair Forest. Almost opposite Yair House stands Fairnilee House, famous as the birthplace in 1712 of Alison Rutherford, a leading member of Edinburgh society in the eighteenth century. She was one of the first to recognize the genius of the then very young Walter Scott. At the same time as Jean Elliot wrote the famous song 'Flowers of the Forest', Alison Rutherford penned another song of the same title. Rutherford's song, however, was no lament for the fallen of Flodden, but referred to the financial misfortunes of many of Ettrick's oldest families in the middle of her own century.

To Ashiestiel and Innerleithen

Junction of Ettrick Water and Tweed (*right*)

Above Ettrick Water Tweed is noticeably narrower and is joined by only minor streams and burns.

Caddon Water flows into Tweed on its north bank, a mile or so up from Fairnilee House. Caddonfoot appears to consist of nothing but a small junior school – presumably the same school that John Leyden, polymath and poet, taught at one summer. It was also at Caddenfoot in 1173 that William the Lion (1143–1214) mustered his army prior to a failed attempt to recover Northumberland. A mile above Caddonfoot lies the hamlet of Clovenfords. The single inn at Clovenfords served Scott as his base in the Borders before he took up residence at Ashiestiel. It was to this inn, which now has a large statue of Scott in front of it, that William and Dorothy Wordsworth went in 1803 to visit the bard – although it was not until the following day at Melrose that they met Scott. Dorothy notes the day in her *Recollections of a Tour made in Scotland*. Of the inn and the reception they received there she wrote: 'a single stone house, without a tree near it or to be seen from it. On our mentioning Mr Scott's name and the woman of the house showed us all possible civility, but her slowness was really amusing. I should suppose it is a house little frequented, for there is no appearance of an inn. Mr Scott, who she told me was a very clever gentleman, "goes there in the fishing season", but indeed Mr Scott is respected everywhere: I believe that by favour of his name one might be hospitably entertained throughout all the borders of Scotland.'

The Wordsworths stayed the night at Clovenfords and it was here that William wrote one of his best known Scottish poems, *Yarrow Unvisited*.

A short way up from Caddonfoot, Tweed is crossed by the Ashiestiel Bridge. A fine and handsome single-span freestone bridge, it was once the largest of its type in Scotland. The view looking upriver from the bridge shows the valley at its autumnal best. The

broadleaf trees beside the tumbling river give way to the massed ranks of conifer that halt only to be crowned by the bare hilltops. Moving clouds throw a constantly changing kaleidoscope of light and shadow over the whole wonderful scene. Across the river on the south bank, partially obscured by the trees, stands the pleasant and well situated Ashiestiel House – the first Border home of Sir Walter Scott. From 1804 until be bought and moved to Abbotsford in 1812, Scott lived, worked and wrote at Ashiestiel. As well as the lease on the house, he also took on a small sheep farm and the sporting rights. At one time Scott considered employing Hogg as his shepherd and bailiff, but chose instead Thomas Purdie, a man whom Scott, in his capacity as sheriff, had recently tried for poaching.

Scott's time at Ashiestiel was both productive and happy. *The Lay of the Last Minstrel, Marmion* and *The Lady of the Lake* were all published during the period of his residence. The great novel *Waverley* was started here. Scott was still a young and healthy man. A keen sportsman and horse rider, he made full use of what nature had so abundantly provided. The beauty of the area and the quality of the river are expressed by a Border poet of a later generation, Andrew Lang (1842–1912), in his *Ballade of the Tweed*:

> There's many a water, great or sma',
> Gaes singing in his siller* tune,
> Through glen and heugh, and hope and shaw
> Beneath the sun-licht or the moan:
> But set us in our fishing-shoon
> Between the Caddon-burn and Peel
> And syne we'll cross the heather brown
> By fair Tweed-side at Ashiestiel.
>
> *silver

Still on the south bank, a couple of miles on from Ashiestiel are the remains of Elibank Castle. Set on high ground back from the river, the ruins are isolated by a few small grassy fields from the massive Elibank and Traquair Forest that surrounds it. The walls that mark out the fields were built and have over the years been repaired with stones taken from the old castle. Not a large structure, it was built around 1600 for Sir Gideon Murry, whose son became the first Lord Elibank in 1643. It was Sir Gideon who is supposed to have married off his singularly ugly daughter, Muckle Mouth Meg, to William Scott, an ancestor of Sir Walter. This William was held in Murry's dungeon and given the choice between wedlock or hanging. At first he opted for the latter but after a further stay in his cell, agreed to matrimony. The true facts of the marriage differ greatly from the story. As with many Border tales, accuracy is not allowed to spoil a good yarn.

Across the river from Elibank and Traquair Forest is the village of Walkerburn. The high hills and craigs behind the village are covered with earthworks and man-made terraces. These date from a very early time and are of more interest to the archaeologist than the historian. There were certainly no signs of recent settlement at the place where Walker Burn enters Tweed when Henry Ballantyne built his village and woollen mills there in the late 1850s. Although designed specifically to serve a single industry, Walkerburn is not an 'ideal town' in the true sense of the term. Its simple, twin-parallel street layout shows none of the thought that went into the planning of later, larger villages such as Lord Leverhulme's Port Sunlight in Cheshire. Ballantyne was very much an industrialist of his time. Always keen to make use of new inventions, he had a hydro-plant built to serve the community's need for power and pumped water.

Less than two miles along the valley and on the same side of the river is Innerleithen. Occupying the only wide section of valley to be found on this section of the river, Innerleithen is equally divided by Leithen Water that enters Tweed just below the town. Mention of the town is made as far back as the twelfth century. King Malcolm IV (1142–65), son of David I, gave Innerleithen Church over to the monks of Kelso. He also granted the church the right of sanctuary, this in thanks for resting the body of his illegitimate son overnight in the church. The boy had drowned in Tweed during a hunting accident. Malcolm IV was known as 'The Maiden', because he never married. As a child of a union not recognized by God, his son's body would not normally have been laid out in a religious house. Claims of an older ecclesiastical connection, between St Rowan and Innerleithen, cannot be substantiated. They were, however, much pro-pounded in the nineteenth century. Innerleithen managed to prosper in the nineteenth century as a most unusual combination of industrial woollen town and spa. It was believed that the spa town in Scott's novel *St Rowan's Well* and Innerleithen were one and the same place. The pump room at Innerleithen is now known as St Rowan's Well; before the publication of Scott's novel it was known more simply as Doo's Well. Whether it was the efficacious waters of the intoxicating countryside, an otherwise serious-minded minister of Innerleithen, James Nicol (1769–1819), was moved to romantic verse:

Where Quair rins sweet among the flowers,
Down by yon woody glen, lassie,
My cottage stand – it shall be yours,
Gin ye will be my ain, lassie.

The gates of Traquair

Across the river from Innerleithen, Tweed is joined by Quair water. The headwater of Quair is high in the glens behind the tiny village of Traquair. These glens and their craigs were once the home of the royal falconry. All that now remains at Traquair is its famous house and a few small cottages. It must at one time have been a lot larger, as prior to the invasion of Edward I (1239–1307), Traquair could appoint its own sheriff. Traquair House or Castle, as it was once known, can be dated back to the tenth century. There is no reason to doubt its claim to be the oldest inhabited house in Scotland.

Scottish kings from David I to Alexander III (1241–86) stayed and held court at Traquair, Mary, Queen of Scots and Darnley (1547–67) stayed and, it is said, 'much argued' there. Indeed there are very few episodes in Border history that did not at some point have a connection with Traquair. That it survived until the Union of the Crowns is surprising. Still more suprising is that the Stuart family, who owned it from 1478, managed to hold both their house and their Catholic faith through the years of Reformation and persecution. The original tenth-century castle forms only a small part of the present house. Additions and enlargements were made to it up until the seventeenth century.

For a house so steeped in well-documented history, it is strange that the true story behind its best-known feature – the Bear Gates, which are permanently closed – should remain a mystery. Both possible explanations date from the eighteenth century and both are equally romantic. Bonnie Prince Charlie (1720–88) rode to and stayed at Traquair in 1745. His aim was to persuade the Earl of Traquair to raise a force to accompany him south to claim the British crown. Reluctantly, the Earl refused, and after the Young Pretender had passed through the gates for the last time, he ordered them to be closed until such time as a Stuart sat once more on the British throne. But a later Earl, the seventh, is also supposed to have had the gates closed. His reason was the sad death of his young wife, the countess. He ordered that the gates be kept shut until 'another countess of Traquair should come to the old house'. If this latter explanation is true, the gates will be closed forever as the line ended with the death of the unmarried eighth Earl in 1861. If the former story is true, then they were not actually the Bear Gates that the young prince rode through. The bears were not mounted on the gate posts until 1747.

For the 6 mi (10 km) from Traquair to Peebles, Tweed's winding course is flanked by trees. The great forests of Cardrona on the south bank and Glentress on the north extend to the skyline.

Peebles: the Beltane Fair

Peebles is an ancient town. There has been some form of settlement on the north bank of Tweed, where Eddleston enters it, since Roman times. The name Peebles is thought to be derived from Pebyel, meaning a collection of tents or sheds. Of the original tent-dwelling settlers nothing remains, except for a few stone artefacts that are occasionally unearthed. Sadly, little also remains of the town it later became. Possibly the oldest structure in the town is the old five-span stone bridge that dates from 1467. But even this was much altered and widened in 1837. Of Peebles Castle nothing survives. The earliest recorded church, dedicated to St Andrew and consecrated in 1195 by Bishop Jocelin within whose Glasgow See Peebles was and remained until the Reformation, exists only as a very fragmented ruin. Remnants of the old Church of the Holy Cross are still visible. This church was built by Alexander III on a site where, in 1261, an ancient stone cross was found, together with the buried, hacked remains of a man. The cross was inscribed with the name Nicholas. As the martyrdom of the third-century St Nicholas had involved his being cut into pieces, the bones were believed to be his. Edward I visited Peebles on his rampage through Scotland. It was not the first and certainly not the last time the town suffered at the hands of an English army. During the centuries of Border Wars, Peebles sustained almost as much damage at the hands of the Scots as of the English. It was not uncommon for Scots to lay waste to the area, either to settle feuds or to cause hardship for the advancing enemy army. These troubles were further compounded by the destructive way of marauding reivers and mosstroopers of later times.

Yet despite its lawless past, Peebles' motto and boast is 'Peebles for Pleasure'. In fairness to the town, it must be said that this is a perfectly reasonable claim based on strong historical fact. From at least the time of William the Lion, the clean air and excellent hunting made Peebles a favoured summer residence. It was the Balmoral of its day. Royal tournaments were held on Kings Muir, just across the river, next to Gallows Hill. One attraction that had drawn people to Peebles since pagan times was the Beltane Fair.

Beltane or Bealtine is Gaelic for 'fire of Boal' and commemorates a time when fires were lit on the tops of hills to the glory of the sun god Boal. The poem 'Peebles, to the Play' is an account of a Beltane fair held in the early part of the fifteenth century. It is firmly believed, especially in Peebles, to have been written by James I of Scotland, the Poet King (1394–1437). This attribution has never been verified. No original manuscript proving authorship has been traced. However, James I may well have been hunting around Peebles on a particular first of May and been moved to chronicle the fair in verse. The long poem is a vivid and graphic description of the festivities, sports and bawdy romance that accompanied the fair. The first verse sets the scene for the revelries to come:

> At Beltane, when ilk body bounds
> To Peebles to the Play
> To hear the singing and the sounds
> Their solace, sooth to say
> By firth and forest forth they found
> They graithit then full gay;
> God wait that wold they do that sound
> For it was their feast-day, they said.

There is still an annual Beltane Fair at Peebles. Although a descendant of the original, it is now held in the third week of June and is combined with the Riding of the Marches, a custom that recalls a time when the people of Peebles rode and inspected the boundaries of their common land. The tradition was started in the sixteenth century and it seems that any breaches in the boundary were summarily dealt with. The present fair and common riding date only from the very end of the nineteenth century. Quite when the old fair stopped is unclear. Certainly in 1608 the resulting bloodshed from disputed bets had led to the banning of horse racing.

More than most other parts of the Borders, Peebles suffered at the hands of Cromwell's men. It was occupied and partially destroyed by troops loyal to Cromwell during their siege of Neidpath Castle.

The early nineteenth century brought calmer conditions. One of the first things mentioned in the entry on the town in Carlisle's *Topographical Directory of Scotland* (1813) is the excellence of its beer. Civilization indeed! By now a thriving agricultural market town, it further prospered with the introduction of woollen industries.

Centuries of changing circumstances and fortunes have left Peebles with many traditions. Inevitably, a place that has had to struggle to survive has acquired a strong individual character. More importantly, it has developed the necessary ability to take full advantage of shifting fashions. The decline in the Borders woollen trade and the move from labour-intensive farming to mechanized methods were both lamented. They were not allowed, however, to send the town into decline. If Peebles could no longer clothe and feed people, it could welcome and entertain them. The holiday trade centred on Peebles and boosted in its early years by the railways is, after all, only continuing a tradition which started with the old kings of Scotland – that of coming to Peebles for pleasure.

Famous sons

Responding to a new demand to satisfy the needs it creates is one of the keys to success. The Peebles-born William Chambers (1800–83) recognized a need for good, intelligent, factual literature inexpensively produced. When he was fourteen, he moved to Edinburgh to start an apprenticeship as a printer. Almost as soon as his training was complete, he began trading as a publisher. Combining high quality and low price, his journals and books were an instant success with the increasingly literate working classes. In 1832 he and his brother Robert (1802–71) established their own publishing firm and the ten volumes of *Chamber's Encyclopaedia* were issued from 1859 to 1868. Although the firm of W. and R. Chambers was based in Edinburgh, William maintained a close association with his native town. Among the works he published was his own authoritative history of the County of Peeblesshire.

Born and educated in Selkirk, Mungo Park (1771–1806?) the African explorer, practised medicine in Peebles. He had already completed one successful expedition to the Dark Continent when he took up practice in the town. A great friend of Scott, whom he entertained with tales of his adventures, he appeared to be settled in the ways of a country doctor. But an offer from the government to lead his own expedition to map the course of Africa's mighty River Niger was more than he could resist. The exact details of this brave man's death will never be known. In his last letter, written after all the other Europeans in the party had perished, he said he would either succeed in his mission or die attempting it. Sadly, the latter proved to be the case.

The trials of Neidpath Castle

A mile or so on from the attractive town of Peebles – the last town on the river – Tweed is watched over by Neidpath Castle. Of all Tweed's many castles, Neidpath most looks to be at one with its position. Set high above the turbulent stream of the narrow river, it appears to have been hewn from the very crags on which it stands. This site on Tweed's north bank has been occupied by a fortress since the twelfth century. The present castle is built around the old one, but has been altered. It is not large, but does not need to be in order to dominate its smaller, tighter valley. The strength of Neidpath was last tested in the seventeenth century by Cromwell's men. Despite assaulting it with some of their finest artillery, they were unable to destroy it.

Many times was Neidpath besieged and battered, but only once was it violated and that was at the hands of one of its owners. William Douglas, fourth Duke of Queensberry, was born in Peebles in 1724. He spent little of his long life (he died in 1810) in Scotland or, for that matter, outside London. He was by all accounts a strong character; his life revolved around gambling – at which he was extremely successful – drinking and womanizing. It was not to satisfy gaming debts, as is often reported, that he had his Scottish estates, including Neidpath, stripped of timber. He cared little for his distant properties; he was a man of the turf and the town. When a girl whom he believed to be his illegitimate daughter was to be married, he decided to provide a dowry. A quick painless means of raising a suitable sum was to sell the oak and other hardwood he owned. How much more beguiling Neidpath would now be had 'Old Q' not removed the terraced garden of trees that once swept down to the river. At the time, he was damned and cursed across the Borders for his philistinism. Although not the most vitriolic attack on the duke, Wordsworth's sonnet *Degenerate Douglas* is, by the author's measure, almost unparalleled in its bile.

> Degenerate Douglas! oh, the unworthy Lord!
> Whom mere despite of heart could so far please,
> And love of havoc, (for with such disease Fame taxes
> Him), that he could send forth word
> To level with the dust a noble horde,
> A brotherhood of venerable Trees,
> Leaving an ancient dome, and towers like these,
> Beggared and outraged! – Many hearts deplored

The fate of those old Trees; and oft with pain
The traveller, at this day, will stop and gaze
On wrongs, which Nature scarcely seems to heed:
For sheltered places, bosoms, nooks, and bays,
And the pure mountains, and the gentle Tweed,
And the green silent pastures, yet remain.

A short way up from Neidpath, Tweed is crossed by a well-engineered rail bridge. Well built but useless. Since the radical rail cuts of the early 1960s, Tweed's towns and villages have learned to rely on roads. The old tracks have all been lifted, the embankments and crossings are slowly being reclaimed by the land; only the bridges remain to remind people of the great days of rail travel.

Above and still within the sight of the old rail bridge, Tweed is joined by Mannor Water. Although not much more than a large stream, it is Tweed's last tributary worth the name.

Fishing

Why do people fish for salmon? What makes the long drive, the expense and the possible discomfort involved in salmon fishing worthwhile? Even the keenest, most optimistic Rod would readily admit that catching a fish is not the primary reason: a visit to a fishmonger is cheaper and more reliable. The oblique answer is that if you are not a fisherman, you will never know. No words can provide the explanation; you have to see for yourself. And nowhere is the answer revealed more convincingly than on the tree-lined beats of the early autumn river. None of the twenty-one beats from Fairnilee Water upstream to Peebles Burgh Water can match their lower river counterparts in terms of fish caught. But what the upper river lacks in fish, it more than compensates for in autumnal beauty.

The Ettrick is Tweed's last great tributary; and from here upstream it is fed by burns. In comparison with the lower river, Tweed, in this initial stretch, might appear fairly large. At Peebles, however, the river is appreciably smaller and more shallow. Even on a high water, it is rare to see boats used on any but the first few beats of this section of river. Rods must therefore get into the water and wade down the pools if they are to fish them effectively. Boats, however necessary on the broad lower Tweed, do create something of a barrier. The wading fisherman is completely at one with his environment.

All rivers stipulate opening and closing dates for their rod-fishing seasons. Rod fishermen on Tweed also have to be aware of those that govern net fishing. Between 15 February and 15 September, any legal method – fly, spinner or worm – can be used to take fish. Outside these dates, only the fly can be used.

A few fish will make their way above Ettrickfoot in the summer; even the odd spring fish will travel this far upriver. But it is with the first equinoctial rains of mid-September that any real number of salmon are seen entering this section. In practice, the first run of fish tends to be of old, potted fish that have spent several months in the lower river. The poor conditions denoted by their dark colour renders these fish of little use for the table and, if caught, they are returned to complete their journey. However, given a good flow of clean water, fresh fish will soon arrive to populate these beats. Whereas Rods on the lower and middle river must look to the watersheds of Teviot and Ettrick as well as upper Tweed to see if their beats are going to run too high for practical fishing, fishermen above Ettrick Mouth need only glance over their shoulders.

The distinctive beauty of this part of Tweed in September and October lies in its colour. The variegated oranges, browns, reds and yellows that clothe the trees along the steep-sided length of the valley are breathtakingly splendid. For the fisherman, every sense is heightened. There is unending pleasure in the sight and sound of the river, the sound of the wind sweeping through the autumn leaves, the song of birds as they flock prior to starting their long migrations, the smell of bonfires and the sight of freshly ploughed fields – and even the occasional taste of success as a fresh salmon is landed. Fishermen, nevertheless, do have to pay a price for this riot of autumn colour. When the leaves finally fall, they seem to find their way into the river. After an early night frost, and assisted by a morning breeze, leaves can be a curse. After almost every cast, Rods are obliged to retrieve their fly to remove the detritus of autumn.

Although the vista of upper Tweed at this time of year is peerless, fishing here, as elswehere, does not come free. The financial value of any stretch of any river is ultimately assessed, however, by the number of fish caught. Consequently, this stretch of river is less expensive to fish than the downstream beats, and quality fishing, in glorious surround-ings, can be enjoyed at an affordable rent. In fact, Peebles Burgh water at the top of this section is controlled by Tweeddale District Council and is available to visiting fishermen at a very modest price.

There is one blot on the near-perfect autumn landscape of this section of upper Tweed

— although, thanks to the efforts of the Tweed Commissioners, it is on the wane. This is the practice of taking fish by a method known as snatching and sniggling. A very high-density, fast-sinking line, armed with a fly carrying a disproportionately large hook, is cast across the river and quickly drawn back, the intention being to foul-hook the fish, i.e. to hook it anywhere but in the mouth. Sadly, this unsporting and cruel method of 'fishing' is still practised by some people not worthy of the term sportsmen.

Newark Castle

Despite its fearsome appearance, Newark Castle was built as a hunting lodge by James II of Scotland. Then it was surrounded by Ettrick Forest; now it is within the Bowhill estate.

An Autumn day (*left*)

A breezy October day shows the upper reaches of Tweed in sumptuous livery.

Ashiestiel House (*right*)

In 1804, shortly after he was appointed sheriff-deputy of Selkirkshire, Scott acquired a house at Ashiestiel so that he could be close to his work, and he lived there until he bought Abbotsford House in 1812.

Yair House (*left*)
This perfectly proportioned and elegant Georgian house stands beside the beautiful and, in the autumn, productive, Yair beat on the upper Tweed.

Sheep on neep (*right*)

In the valley of Eddleston Water colder weather and exhausted pastures mean that sheep must be brought down to feed on the neep.

The Hogg Monument (*left*)

James Hogg, the Ettrick
shepherd, sits with his dog
beside him overlooking
St Mary's Loch.

Yair Bridge (*right*)

The subtle shades of autumn
run down to the banks of the
river. This is the first bridge
above Tweed's confluence
with Ettrick Water.

Elibank Castle (*left*)

The crumbling remains of the early seventeenth-century castle are surrounded by a dry stone wall that was undoubtedly built in part from stone removed from the castle ruins.

Walkerburn (*right*)

Built exclusively as a mill village, Walkerburn stands beside Tweed, its source of power. In an area where flat land is at a premium, a rugby pitch takes precedence over crops.

Box loom (*left*)

Before the advent of powered factories, weaving was carried out as a cottage industry. This reconstructed interior and original loom are housed in the Scottish Museum of Woollen Textiles at Walkerburn.

Traquair House (*right*)

Believed to be the oldest inhabited house in Scotland, Traquair dates from the tenth century. The 'new' wings were added in 1680.

Innerleithen (*overleaf*)

The mill town and spa is situated on Leithen Water, near its junction with Tweed, on one of the few plains to be found on the upper river. Poor drainage makes the land susceptible to flooding in times of heavy rain.

The Bear Gates (*left*)

The permanently closed entrance to Traquair House is also known as the Steekit Yetts. One tradition maintains that on the departure of Bonnie Prince Charlie, the gates were closed by the fifth Earl, who vowed that they would not be re-opened until a Stuart again sat on the British throne.

Kailzie Gardens (*right*)

A few miles downriver from Peebles are the arboretum and garden of the now sadly demolished Kailzie House. At over 600 ft (200 m) above sea level, the plants are limited to those that can tolerate the altitude and the chill north-east prospect.

Peebles (*left*)

Of the five spans of Peebles Bridge, two are used only when persistent heavy rain raises the level of Tweed to flood height. The Kirk is the most recent of the town's churches.

Peebles Hydro (*right*)

The huge, French château-like hotel stands, rather incongruously, in the conifer plantations above Tweed's valley.

Neidpath Castle (*left*)

This fourteenth-century tower house is defended on three sides by Tweed and was further fortified by walls that are 12 ft (3.7 m) thick.

St Mary's Loch (*right*)

At the head of Yarrow Water, which enters the Ettrick just above Selkirk, is the largest loch in southern Scotland. Sir Walter Scott used to fish for trout here.

LATE AUTUMN

Mannor Bridge to Tweed's Well

Stobo Kirk (1) • *Stobo Castle (2)* • *Drumelzier Plain (3)* • *Merlindale Bridge (4)*
Stanhope (5) • *Crook Inn (6)* • *Tweedsmuir Kirk (7)*
Tweedsmuir Bridge (8) • *Sheepdog Centre (9)* • *Source of Tweed (10)*

Above Tweedsmuir

The young river pushes and twists its way through the cold, bleak countryside of late autumn.

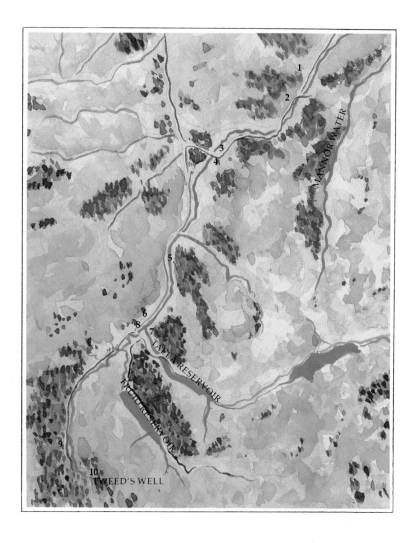

THE CLOSING MONTHS OF THE YEAR ARE THE TIME TO VISIT the fine section of Tweed from its source at Tweed's Well to Mannor Bridge. The distance between the start of the Tweed and Mannor is a little over 23 mi (37 km). They are steep and hilly miles. During the course of this section, the rushing, tumbling, impatient stream falls nearly two-thirds of its 1500-ft (500-m) descent to the sea. This is hard country; in many ways inhospitable. Population is sparse and the few people who do live along Tweed's narrow banks are congregated in the tiny villages found at the lower end of the section.

From man's earliest occupation of Tweed and its valleys, Mannor Water appears to have been as far upriver as any widespread settlements were made. There are more archaeological sites dating from the Iron Age (c1200–100 BC) to be found along Mannor's short valley than beside all of the rest of this stretch of upper river, and some remnants of prehistoric cultures – standing stones, hill forts and homesteads – can still be made out.

Prior to the recent introduction of good road communications, this wild area was primarily known for its lawlessness. It must be remembered that terms such as 'Dark Ages' and 'Middle Ages' refer more to stages of development, levels of civilization and artistic advance, than to periods strictly bounded by dates. It is therefore safe to say that at the same time as the Italian republics and courts were glorying in the Renaissance, northern Britain was struggling to come to terms with a medieval way of life. The more isolated an area, the less advanced its government. The time and effort required to impose law on the always small numbers of people living in upper Tweeddale left the administration of law and order largely in the hands of local lairds or clan chiefs. For centuries, only large-scale insurrection against the Crown or influential neighbours brought the influence of national law and order to the district.

Until the early years of the twentieth century, drovers used to be employed to bring cows and sheep down out of Scotland, either to lower, warmer pastures or to English livestock sales. These autumn migrations of men and beasts were at constant risk when travelling through upper Tweeddale. Many a drover left the valley with a depleted herd or empty purse, and some poor souls did not leave at all. Today, the only remnant of this lawlessness in the district is, sadly, the poaching of salmon from the river.

The appearance of Tweed's upper valley has changed greatly over the centuries as a result of human intervention. Five hundred years ago the lower half of the late autumn river was surrounded by forest, while most of the upper half was moorland and heath. The forest, as with most of the great ancient woodland beside Tweed, was not a uniform, dense canopy of hardwood. The higher crags would have been dotted with juniper, thorn, hazel, rowan and birch while the valleys would have contained a denser mix of alder, ash, willow, Scots pine and oak. It was this diversity of species and density that made the forests such good hunting grounds. As well as the grouse, pheasant and hare which still abound in the area, bears, wolves and wild boar once lived and thrived in this forest kingdom. It was in an attempt to deprive the mosstroopers and freebooters of cover that the forest clearances first began in earnest. As a result of the reduction in woodland, more grazing for sheep became available. The increased revenue from wool and mutton then led to the further and finally near-total destruction of the forest lands.

By the start of this century, with the exception of a few small woods, the whole area was either heath, heather or grass. Unlike the rich pasture and fertile land to be found further down Tweed, this upland district has to count acres per sheep, not sheep per acre. Tweeddale farmers and shepherds had, and still have, to travel far and work hard to make a living from the land. In the summer months, the flocks are driven up to the higher hills to feed on the short-lived mountain grasses. In autumn they must be brought down to the sweeter meadows. Winter can find the shepherds digging their animals out of snowdrifts or waist-deep in water retrieving them from swollen burns. At lambing time the shepherd will get little or no sleep. Long days and nights are spent tending the ewes and caring for orphaned and abandoned lambs. With sons unwilling to follow their fathers on to the hills and farmers getting only a poor return, the relatively high land prices offered and accepted from the Forestry Commission are encouraging a move away from sheep-farming.

The nineteenth-century Romantics damned the Duke of Queensberry for denuding Neidpath of its oaks because they felt that the removal robbed the site of some of its natural beauty. It is probably true to say that they would feel much the same way about the vast conifer plantations of upper Tweeddale. The massed black ranks of pines are increasingly covering the hills. Their darkness and density flattens and hides the shape and feature of the land. Unlike the forests of Traquair, Cardrona, Elibank and Ettrick, their edges are not softened by broadleaf species. They start and finish with abrupt and jarring lines. As well as being somewhat incongruous, these plantations, or rather the drainage associated with them, have changed the nature of Tweed's flow. When rain falls on the bare or naturally planted hills, it is absorbed into the land. The water is then slowly released into the river system. With land that is systematically drained, the run-off is almost instant. As a result the river can rise and fall with alarming speed, shifting the salmon redds and smothering them with the increased amount of suspended matter. Tweed's softwood forests do, of course, have an economic role to play in the area. Over

100,000 tonnes of timber are cropped from them each year, most of the wood going either for use in building work or to be pulped for papermaking. Wherever possible, crops are still grown, mainly just beside the river. But, for the most part, the land is not suitable for arable use. With the exception of bare craigs and scree, any land that is not used for sheep or given over to plantation is covered with heather. The heather moorlands occupy ground that would be perfectly suited to either tree plantation or grazing. Were it not for the red grouse, this would undoubtedly be their fate; the moors would be lost forever.

The costs of shooting

The major country sports are shooting and fishing, and it is fishing that makes the least demands on the land. A steady, uninterrupted flow of clean water, free of pollutants, is the only requirement for maintaining a suitable habitat for fish. A river has no other value than as a river; its course, the riverbed, cannot be put to any other use. Shooting, on the other hand, requires land to be set aside. Spinneys and coverts, hedges and scrub, woods and ponds have to be maintained and preserved. Game crops free from non-selective pesticides must be planted. Broad rides and sheltered feeding areas in large woods have to be established. In order to provide the necessary habitat for the successful rearing and management of game, otherwise profitable land must be surrendered. In Britain as a whole, much of the appeal of the countryside lies in its diverse appearance. Huge open fields, broken only by tractor tracks and wire fences, would indeed be a dull sight. Were it not for the interests of shooting, such vistas would be monotonously common. Farmers are, of course, in business; their livelihoods depend on the use to which they put their land. When catering for the needs of shooting, farmers must either bear the loss of income from arable or livestock production themselves (as a good many do) or be paid for doing so. To give an idea of the cost of pheasant shooting, there is an old (but constantly updated) saying: 'Up goes ten pounds, bang goes twenty pence, down comes one pound fifty'. The ten pounds is the cost of rearing, feeding and supplying the bird with a suitable habitat (including an allowance for the birds that are not shot), the twenty pence is the cost of a cartridge, and one pound fifty the market value of the pheasant.

Provided suitable provisions are made, partridge and pheasant shooting may be carried out within a farming system. Grouse, on the other hand, must be allowed the sole use of the land, with the exception of perhaps a few sheep grazing on the heather margins. The amount of land required for a grouse moor is vast. It is measured in thousands rather than hundreds of acres. When the gamekeepers assess the stock of birds on the moor in spring, they calculate them as the number of breeding pairs per 200 acres; thirty-five pairs would be considered a dense population. The red grouse (*Lagopus scoticus*) is the only species of bird peculiar to Britain. Although an extremely hardy bird – it can survive conditions ranging from snow to drought – it does demand the exclusive habitat provided by the heather moorland. The diet of the mature birds consists of the young shoots of heather, while the chicks feed on the insects that proliferate on the heather. Paradoxically, it requires careful and constant management to keep a heather moor in optimum natural condition. Left to their own devices, the heather bushes would become old and leggy until they eventually died. In time, the moor would undergo some rejuvenation; however, during the years of decline and emptiness, the grouse would be denied large areas of feeding and cover. It is therefore necessary to monitor the condition of the heather and, when it starts to show signs of ageing, to burn it back, allowing new, healthy plants to shoot up and replace the old stock. During this process, the grouse, together with the myriad other creatures that occupy the moor, have the good sense to get out of the path of the fire and move to safer parts of the moor.

Grouse shooting, probably even more than salmon fishing, is thought of as a rich man's sport. Certainly the tweed-clad Guns that occupy the butts on the premier moors are paying handsomely for the privilege. But just as salmon fishing can be had on lesser beats of great rivers at a relatively modest cost, so some grouse shooting is available at a moderate price. Driven grouse, whereby Guns are stationed in butts having birds driven over them by small armies of beaters, may cost the Guns an unspeakable amount of money. On the other hand, walked-up shooting, involving a line of Guns accompanied only by dogs walking across the moor and flushing birds as they go, is comparatively inexpensive. Well-kept grouse moors have many more beneficiaries than the small number of people to be found in the butts on the Glorious Twelfth of August, when the grouse-shooting season opens. The moor is home to countless species of birds and animals, as well as insects and butterflies. Local people – keepers, beaters and hoteliers – all make a living from the moors. For the wider public, the glorious sight of a vast heather moor in full bloom, or the intricate tapestry of colours seen throughout the rest of the year, add immeasurably to the beauty of Britain's upland areas.

Tweed and Lyne

From Mannor to Berwick, Tweed's course continues through a splendid variety of countryside, sometimes broad and open, sometimes soft and hilly. But always, the nature of its surroundings is reflected in the river itself. In this final section, the valley is steep and the hills are high. Thus, in the descent to Mannor the river is narrow and purposeful.

A couple of miles up from Mannor Water, Tweed is joined from the north by Lyne Water. A short way up the valley of the Lyne is the small and very pretty village of the same name. Beyond the village where Lyne is joined by Tarth Burn stand the forlorn ruins of Drochil Castle. It was built but never completed for James Douglas, Earl of Morton. James, who during the middle years of the sixteenth century had played a crucial and often cruel role at court, desired for himself a grand country retreat where he could escape the affairs of the nation. It was he who brought the plans for a contraption called the Maiden (an early guillotine) to Scotland. This machine, so efficient at beheading people, was to be used on the laird of Pennecuick, but he managed to beat the Maiden by dying in bed. The earl was not so fortunate. In 1581, three years after building began on his castle, James was involved in the murder of the Earl of Darnley and became the Maiden's first victim. Such are the ironies of life.

The ground between Tweed and Lyne is known as Sheriff Muir. William Wallace (c1270–1305) was supposed to have been involved in a small engagement there. Certainly in later years the Muir was the muster and parade ground for the local militia.

From Lyne Water, Tweed can be followed on the B712 – first on its north bank as far as Dawyck, where it crosses the river, and then skirting the south bank until it crosses back at Drumelzier. A mile north of Drumelzier, the minor road joins the A701, the main Edinburgh-Dumfries road. After the mile or so it takes to rejoin the river, the main road stays within a few hundred yards of Tweed all the way to the source.

Upper Tweeddale

The first of the settlements of upper Tweeddale (they are too small to be called villages) is Stobo. The name Stobo, which has over the years had almost as many spellings as occupants, comes from the Gaelic and means 'the hollow of stumps'. This recalls the time when it formed part of a huge ancient forest. A more tangible reminder of a long-gone age is Stobo Kirk, the only surviving medieval church in Peeblesshire. Additions were made to it – the south porch and west chapel, although still medieval, are of a later date. One unusual feature of the church is its lack of carved decoration. It is likely that the masonry was at one time decoratively inscribed, but then the post-Reformation taste for plain houses of worship prevailed and the old carving would have been removed. A little beyond Stobo Kirk stands Stobo Castle. It was built between 1805 and 1811 to a design by Archibald and James Elliot for Sir James Montgomery. The Montgomerys were a legal family – the first Sir James who bought the land in 1867 was Lord Advocate of Scotland and later Lord Chief Baron of the Scottish Exchequer. His son, the second Sir James of Stobo, who commissioned the castle, was also Lord Advocate of Scotland although he resigned the post after only two years in office. The castle is a particularly fine Georgian mansion in the Gothick style pioneered by Horace Walpole in the late eigtheenth century. Despite its external towers and castellations, the interior is very much in the classical tradition and the entrance hall and staircase are illuminated by a grand glass cupola. Stobo Castle remained in the hands of the Montgomerys until the unfortunate death of the last Sir James, who fell from a speeding night express train to London in 1903. The castle is now used as a private health and beauty spa.

Dawyck and Drumelzier

Within sight of Stobo, across the river on the south bank, are Dawyck Botanic Gardens, which form the arboretum of the Royal Botanic Gardens of Edinburgh. The gardens are planted and laid out within the grounds of the old Dawyck House. Here, too, are also the ruins of the even older Dawyck Church, now almost lost among the trees. Dawyck was for many centuries owned by that redoubtable border family, the Veitches. From the twelfth until the early eighteenth century, they fought for, owned, disputed and claimed the land around Tweeddale. Their power was in strength, not learning. It was not until the end of the fifteenth century that a Veitch mastered the art of writing his own name.

The variety of species found at Dawyck befits a national collection. The first horse chestnuts in Scotland were planted here in 1650; the first larches in 1725. If Alexander Pennecuick is to be believed, Dawyck once had some most extraordinary pear trees. In his book *Description of Tweeddale* (1715), he tells of trees that bear flesh, fish and fruit. Herons returning to their nests among the fruiting pear trees would devour whole fish

Stobo Kirk (*left*)

The oldest church in
Tweeddale, Stobo Kirk is
Norman with later additions.
A stained-glass window in
the side chapel depicts
Merlin's supposed conversion
to Christianity by St Mungo.

Stobo Castle (*right*)

The castle was designed by
James Elliot, the Edinburgh-
based architect, in the Gothic
Revival style.

they had caught from Tweed. These fish passed through the birds intact and slithered down the tree to the ground!

From Dawyck, Tweed's valley on the south bank opens into Drumelzier Plain. Drumelzier is one of the many Gaelic names to be found in this area. Its meaning is something of an exclamation: 'Here is a plain!'. In fact, it is the only sizeable area of flat ground to be found along Tweed's course after Kelso. The rich alluvial soil is farmed in a systematic way that looks almost out of place in this otherwise wild and hilly region. Overlooking the neat plain and the river beyond are the ragged remains of Tinnis Castle. Erected within the grounds of an Iron Age fort, Tinnis's once-mighty walls measured 88 ft (27 m) by 75 ft (23 m). Built sometime around the end of the fifteenth century, it was home and bastion of the Tweedie family. The name was said to allude to the family having descended directly from the river's water spirits, and the Tweedies did certainly try to make this part of Tweed their own. Over the centuries of occupation in the area, their name became synonymous with lawlessness and violence. The truth is that they were probably no worse than other local lairds, with whom they constantly feuded. Tinnis is said to have been blown up by one of their enemies, the Flemings. Although no documentary evidence exists to confirm this, the completeness of the destruction and the range at which fragments of the castle have been found suggest more than a mere artillery attack.

The few houses that form Drumelzier stand alongside Powsail (Drumelzier) Burn, which enters Tweed just where the flat lands begin to surrender to the hills. It is between the river and the burn that the great Caledonian wizard, Merlin, is said to be buried. After his final battle, in which his pagan forces fought with and lost to King Arthur's Christian faithful, Merlin retired broken and mad to upper Tweeddale. Deranged and ranting, he wandered the forest until finally he was set upon, stoned and staked by a band of shepherds who buried him near to where he fell. The poet and prophet of a later, but equally mysterious age, Thomas the Rymer, prophesied:

When Tweed, and Powsail, meet at Merlins grave
Scotland and England shall one Monarch have.

Strangely enough, on the day that James VI (1566–1625) was crowned James I of England, a mighty flood came down Tweed, bursting its banks and causing it to overflow and mix with the lower end of Powsail Burn. A stained-glass window in Stobo Church tells of a happier end to Merlin's troubles. It depicts him kneeling before St Mungo, having renounced his heathen ways in favour of the Christian faith.

Above Drumelzier, Tweed is crossed by the modern Merlindale Bridge, a low metal structure that hardly lives up to the romance of its name. It does, however, afford splendid views upstream and downstream. At this point, the road deviates from the river around Rachan Hill, the top of which is crowned by the few remaining stones of the old fort. The now dismantled railway line that once ran the length of the upper river was not as timid as the road and followed hard by the river. After Rachan Hill, Tweed passes the remains of two of its last Peel towers – Wrae Farm Tower on the north bank and Drumelzier Place Tower on the south. Now all but gone, they represent the upper end of a system of communication that was once capable of sending a message of impending danger over 80 mi (130 km) along the river at the speed of light.

This part of Tweed abounds with sites, ruins and remains. Ever since the valley was first occupied, people have built and destroyed, creating and abandoning farmsteads, forts, castles, towers, churches and graveyards. A few later structures survive, but for the most part the wilful desire to destroy finally overcame the efforts of the urge to create. The one exception to this is provided by the simple, domestic homes. That no such dwelling survives from an earlier period than the end of the eighteenth century is due to natural rather than human destruction. Despite the endlessly available supply of stones, the people of this cold country chose turf as their building material. What these dark and often damp homes lacked in strength, they more than compensated for in warmth. The walls were buttressed with wood and the roofs were made of timber overlaid with earth. When the cruel elements began to rot and wash away the home, a new one would be built and nature allowed to reclaim the materials of the old one.

Above Stanhope Burn, which enters Tweed on the north bank, the river loses any pretensions it may have held to be anything other than a highland stream, one of a number which tumble down from the high moorland landscape. Polmood Burn joins Tweed at Polmood House, one-time home of the Hunter family. Well beyond the middle of the eighteenth century, Hunter of Polmood was recognized head of his own clan. On the death of the last undisputed clan leader, the intricacies of the inheritance of the title led many of that name to court. A century or two earlier the claim would have been settled by the sword. But these were civilized times. Lawyers were employed, records consulted and lost (probably fictitious) deeds were cited. The whole case, which makes Jarndyce and Jarndyce in Dickens's *Bleak House* seem as trivial as a disputed present-day parking offence, dragged on for over forty years. The claim was finally settled to the satisfaction of one Hunter and no doubt to a vast number of lawyers.

Less than a mile up and across the river from Polmood is the old and most welcome

Crook Inn. Most welcome as it is the only inn between Moffat and Peebles. Originally a seventeenth-century coaching inn, it takes its name from the hook, or crook, that used to be suspended by a chain over the fire on which cooking pots could be hung. Among the more illustrious guests to have supped at the Crook Inn were Walter Scott and his circle; before them, Robert Burns (1759–96) was known to have written poetry while sitting at the Crook's kitchen table. In the early eighteenth century there were three other inns along this road. One of them, the Bield, was built in 1700 specifically for cadgers. They were the itinerant merchants who travelled through the country areas buying produce to resell in the town. The modern association of their name is obviously not new; the Bield was built because none of the other local inns was prepared to accommodate the cadgers.

On the same side as the Crook Inn and across the river from the half-dozen houses and church that form Tweedsmuir is the site of Oliver's Castle. A site so bare as to be almost impossible to distinguish, it would not be worth consideration were it not for its former occupants. The Frasers of Tweedsmuir were descended from a French family. Quite when they settled in the Borders and how they came to power is not clear. That they were Peeblesshire's strongest family at the end of the thirteenth century is beyond doubt. Oliver's Castle was probably built some time in the twelfth century by Oliver Fraser, but it is a later member of the family, Simon Fraser, whose life is best documented. As well as his own career, we can get an insight into the ways and loyalties of the baronial lords of Britain at the turn of the fourteenth century. Having sworn allegiance to Edward I in 1296, Simon Fraser was appointed Keeper of Ettrick Forest in 1300. In 1302 he defected from Edward's service, leaving Wark Castle with a quantity of armour and horses to join William Wallace. A year later he sided with the Red Comyn at the battle of Roslyn where 10,000 Scots defeated 30,000 English – at that time Robert Bruce was fighting *with* the English. In February 1304 Comyn and Fraser laid down their arms, and Fraser was sent into exile for four years. He returned to Scotland after two of these and joined Bruce's uprising. Shortly after, he was captured by the English, taken to London and executed. Although Frasers occupied parts of Tweeddale for another 300 years, they never regained the power they had once enjoyed.

The Covenanters of Tweedsmuir

Tweedsmuir stands on Tweed's south bank, between the river and Talla Water, the second of its main tributaries in this upland section. Some 2 mi (3 km) upstream from its mouth, Talla has been dammed to form Talla Reservoir, part of the Edinburgh water supply system. Although few in number, the homes at Tweedsmuir represent the first grouping of houses to be found on Tweed. The pretty little kirk at Tweedsmuir is relatively new, having been built in 1874, although during its short life its congregation has slowly dwindled. Its predecessor, however, saw much crueller events. Some of the gravestones in the peaceful churchyard mark the final resting place of those men of Tweeddale killed during the Covenant Wars of the 1680s. The Covenanters were a group of free Protestants who refused to bow to a single centrally-imposed form of Christian worship, arguing that to do so not only denied them and others freedom of choice, but also allowed government control of the Church in the name of the King. In 1682 a Covenanter's conference was held at Talla Lins, a wild and secluded spot up the Talla valley. Although it lasted for three days, very little was achieved, most of the time being taken up with doctrinal arguments. Covenanters' meetings and the Covenanters themselves were at constant risk from the king's dragoons. John Graham of Claverhouse was strictly only sheriff of Galloway, Dumfries and Annandale, but he sent his dragoons into Tweeddale to kill any Covenanters they might find. The right of freedom of religion was eventually granted, and the Covenanter cause could be said to have been won. But the price was high and the years of oppression are still known as the 'killing time'. Memories are long in this part of the Borders. Until the end of the last century, hill shepherds would destroy peewits' nests and kill their young as they believed that the song of the birds had given away the hiding place of many fugitive Covenanters.

Above Talla Water and Tweed's next sizeable tributary – Fruid Water, also dammed to supply Edinburgh's taps – is the site of the Giant's Grave. There was at one time in the area an inexplicable belief in giants. Tales abounded of the goliaths of Tweedsmuir. Just when the incumbent of this particular grave was lowered into the cavernous hole in the ground is unknown.

In its last 6 mi (10 km) above Fruid Water, Tweed is fed by a series of small burns. They are enough to keep the young river alive, but not strong enough to sustain much growth. The need to bridge the river was left behind at Tweedsmuir. From here to its source Tweed can easily be crossed, first with stepping stones, then with a single stepping stone, then by a leap and, finally, almost dismissively, in a single stride.

Tweed begins its life where we finish this journey, at a small unmarked well – Tweed's Well.

Fishing

The Tweed valley upriver of Mannor Water can be most attractive. It can be grand, it can be fascinating and, in the closing weeks of Novenber, it can be downright inhospitable.

This last section of river is, for both fish and fishermen, by far the steepest. Long gone are the slow, lazy pools of the lower river. No more can fish make their way, swimming against a gentle flow. Forgotten are the Rods' sedentary days spent in a boat. Fish must work hard to push their way up through the fast tumbling water to find suitable breeding grounds. Fishermen need to be sure-footed, initially to reach and then to fish the small, boulder-strewn river. In early autumn, a shirt and jacket were sufficient protection against a chill in the air. Now the thermal clothing that was packed away in spring has to be taken out again. The high, wispy cloud of balmier days is replaced by dark, heavy cloud that fills the valley and obscures the hills. During the dry months of summer, the top river was reduced to a benign, babbling stream. Now the rain and sleet that herald the onset of winter turn the stream into an angry torrent.

Salmon return to the river to spawn, or rather, they return to the river system. Some fish will form redds barely above the high-tide mark; others will head for the many tributaries and burns along Tweed's length. Considering the number of fish that enter the system, very few will struggle the full 90 mi (140 km) upstream to channel out an area of gravel and thus start the cycle over again.

A small number of fish will have used the summer floods to travel above Mannor Bridge earlier in the year. But, as a rule, it is only following several high autumn floods that fish begin to appear this far upriver. The lower and middle river beats of Tweed hold out a good hope of fish throughout the ten months of the season. The river from Ettrick to Mannor receives most attention from fishermen between September and November. Depending on weather conditions, this top river can have an effective season of one month or even less. Not that its banks are completely neglected by fishermen in the summer. Trout fishermen, using short, light rods and small flies (which, unlike the creations used by salmon fishers, are true imitations), will be out in pursuit of the succulent and sporting Tweed trout.

Although hardly recognizable as such, this is the River Tweed and Rods are thus still obliged to comply with the fly-only rule at this period of late autumn. The need for the long rods of 15 ft (5 m) and over that are used lower downriver is fast diminishing. Somewhat shorter rods and lighter lines are now quite capable of covering and fishing the water effectively. Flies no longer need to be so large or heavy. The fish that are caught between Mannor Water and Tweedsmuir, the highest point worth fishing, are never fresh. At best they will be a little coloured, having spent a time in the river. Any fresh-looking fish is bound to be exhausted. Most fish at this time of year and this far up the system will be dark and ripe, i.e. just about to spawn. Consequently, a large percentage of fish caught are quickly and safely returned to the river.

Fishing this far up river is frequently cold, hard, unrewarding work. When not cloaked in cloud, however, the scenery is magnificent, the air is clean and clear and, most importantly of all, it is fishing and it is Tweed.

Modern fishing flies

A selection of various sizes and weights to cover different water heights and temperatures. Modern flies are not as ornate as their Victorian and Edwardian counterparts, but are no less effective.

Drumelzier plain (*left*)

Merlin is said to be buried between the plain and Drumelzier Burn. From here, the flat land gives way to the hills, and signs of habitation become increasingly scarce.

Merlindale Bridge (*right*)

The new Bailey bridge-type construction at the top end of Drumelzier Plain reflects the rugged nature of the land.

The Crook Inn (*left*)

The inn has entertained many illustrious literary guests in the last 350 years, and it is still a welcome sight to travellers on the high road that accompanies Tweed to its source.

The Crook Inn: interior
(*right*)

The perfectly preserved Art Deco interior within the eighteenth-century hotel is as wonderful as it is unexpected. The whole building was refitted when it was bought as a wedding anniversary present for the wife of a Glasgow shipbuilder in the 1920s.

John Hunter's grave (*left*)

The graveyard of Tweedsmuir Kirk contains the only graves of Covenanters to be found along Tweed's entire length. In the late seventeenth century the area around Tweedsmuir and Talla teemed with Covenanter activity.

Tweedsmuir Kirk (*right*)

Set among the high hills near to the source of Tweed, the present kirk, which was built in 1874, serves the spiritual needs of the people of this beautiful but unforgiving area just as its predecessors had done.

Talla reservoir (*left*)

The reservoir was formed by the damming of Talla Water, one of Tweed's upper tributaries. By the time it was opened in the early years of this century, many men had lost their lives in its construction.

Fruid reservoir (*right*)

The stark utilitarian lines of the run-off date the reservoir's construction firmly in the last half of the twentieth century.

A Borders shepherdess
(*left*)

Old shepherding skills are kept alive by Viv Billingham, who, with her husband, runs the Tweed Hill Foot Farm as a sheepdog centre. Attempts to preserve the traditional life style have been made increasingly urgent by the steady encroachment of the conifer plantations.

Border collie penning sheep (*right*)

A good dog has always been the shepherd's essential partner and best friend.

Tree planting (*left*)

Plastic tubes are used to protect tender young trees. From a distance the hillsides look like war cemeteries.

Heather burning (*right*)

Until recently Stanhope Burn Farm was a sheep station. The heather has to be burned if a healthy moor is to be maintained and the grouse stock re-established.

Sheep and snow (*overleaf*)

Black-faced sheep make the most of what grazing is available in the early snow. As the weather worsens, the flocks are moved down to lower pastures.

Old Road Bridge above Ettrick Foot (*left*)

The old bridge has been made redundant by the new road bridge carrying the A7 from Galashiels to Selkirk.

Source of Tweed (*right*)

The boggy upland hillside from which the river springs stands 1,500 ft (450 m) above Berwick, which is almost 100 river miles (160 km) away.

BIBLIOGRAPHY

Bennett, J., *Companion to Tweed*. Edinburgh, 1938

Buchan, John, *Scholar Gipsies*. London, Bodley Head, 1896

Chambers, W., *History of Peeblesshire*. Chambers, 1864

Cooper, John Ashley, *The Great Salmon Rivers of Scotland*. Witherby, 1987

Crockett, W. S., *In Border Country*. Edinburgh, 1905

Eddington, Alexander, *Castles & Historic Homes of the Border*. 1926

Finley, Gerald, *Landscapes of Memory*. Scolar Press, 1980

Gillies, V., Steel, J., Klein, S., *Tweed Journey*. Canongate, 1989

Grimble, A., *Salmon Rivers of Scotland*. Edinburgh, 1913

Jeffrey, Alexander, *History and Antiquities of Roxburghshire*. Edinburgh, 1855

Lauder, Sir Thomas Dick, *Scottish Rivers*. Edinburgh, 1874

Maxwell, H., *The Story of the Tweed*. Edinburgh/London, 1905

Mills, D. (ed.), *Tweed Towards 2000*. Tweed Foundation, 1989

Mills, D., Graesser, N., *The Salmon Rivers of Scotland*. Cassell, 1981 (new ed. 1992)

The New Statistical Account of Scotland. Edinburgh, 1840

Pennecuik, Alexander, *Description of Tweeddale*. 1815

Ridpath, George, *The Border-History of England and Scotland, to the Union*.
    Edinburgh, 1776

Royal Commission Inventories:
    County of Berwick (1915) Edinburgh, HMSO
    County of Roxburgh (1956) Edinburgh, HMSO
    County of Selkirk (1957) Edinburgh, HMSO
    Peeblesshire (1967) Edinburgh, HMSO

Scott, John, *Berwick-upon-Tweed*. Edinburgh, 1888

Scott, Sir Walter, *Border Antiquities of England and Scotland* Vols I & II.
    Edinburgh, 1814–1817

—*Border Ballads*. Edinburgh

—*Journal of Sir Walter Scott*. (ed. W. E. K. Anderson), Edinburgh

—*Minstrelsy of the Scottish Border*. Edinburgh

—*Poetical Works.* Edinburgh, 1857

Scrope, W., *Days and Nights of Salmon Fishing in the Tweed.* 1843

Stoddart, T., *An Angler's Rambles and Angling Songs.* Edinburgh, 1866

Stoddart, T., *The Angler's Companion to the Rivers and Lochs of Scotland.* Edinburgh,
    1847

Thorndike, Lynn, *Michael Scott.* Nelson, London, 1965

Thornton, T., *A Sporting Tour through the Northern Part of England & Great Part of
    the Highlands of Scotland.* 1896

Veitch, John, *History & Poetry of the Scottish Border.* Edinburgh, 1893

Younger, John *River Angling for Salmon & Trout.* Kelso, 1864

INDEX

Page references in *italics* refer to captions

BORDERS HOUSES AND MONUMENTS OPEN TO THE PUBLIC

Please note that many of the houses and sites mentioned in this book are in private hands and are *not* open to the public. The following may be visited, but opening times and admission charges should be checked with the Scottish Tourist Board, or local Tourist Information Centres.

ABBEYS

Dryburgh
Jedburgh
Kelso
Melrose

GARDENS

Bemersyde
Dawyck
The Hirsel
Kailzie
Mertoun

HOUSES

Abbotsford
Bowhill
Floors Castle
Mellerstain
Niedpath
Paxton
Smailholm Tower
Traquair

TOURIST INFORMATION CENTRES

Coldstream
Henderson Parks
0890 2607

Jedburgh
Murray's Green
0835 63435

Peebles
Chambers Institute
0721 20138

Eyemouth
Auld Kirk, Manse Road
08907 50678

Kelso
Turret House
0573 23464

The Scottish Tourist Board
23 Ravelston Terrace
Edinburgh EH4 3EV
031 332 2433

Galashiels
Bank Street
0896 55551

Melrose
Priorwood Gardens
089682 2555